NORMAN DOMESTIC
AR

Margaret Wood

LONDON 1974

THE ROYAL ARCHAEOLOGICAL INSTITUTE

ROYAL ARCHAEOLOGICAL INSTITUTE
MONOGRAPHS

Editor: M. J. Swanton

The present study is an augmented and revised version of a paper which originally appeared in *The Archaeological Journal* XCII (for 1935)

ISBN 0 903986 02 7

Printed in Great Britain by W. S. Maney & Son Ltd, Leeds, England

CONTENTS

LIST OF PLATES

PREFACE

Since the publication of 'Norman Domestic Architecture'[1] in 1935 more examples have been found, some revealed by bombing or demolition, such as the house off the Stonegate at York and the chimney from 79½ High Street, Southampton. Others have been exposed through excavation, notably at Cheddar in Somerset where P. A. Rahtz has uncovered no less than four royal halls dating from the ninth to thirteenth centuries. In Winchester Martin Biddle's excavations in Lower Brook Street show that the earliest houses (of wood) date from the eleventh century, and a more substantial stone house of c. 1125 retains loop windows in what was presumably the undercroft of a first-floor hall, the entrance being in an end wall, with nearby evidence of an internal staircase to the hall above.[2] This may be compared with the manor house of 1180–90 at Wharram Percy in Yorkshire, excavated by J. G. Hurst and the Deserted Medieval Village Research Group.

Of equal importance is the new light thrown on buildings already cited, chiefly by the Ministry of Public Buildings and Works, now the Department of the Environment. Of highest interest are the fortified palaces of the two great building bishops of the twelfth century, Roger, Bishop of Salisbury (1101–39), and Henry of Blois, Bishop of Winchester (1129–71), the wealthy brother of King Stephen. Sherborne Old Castle was built by Roger of Sarum between 1107 and 1135. It has a central courtyard with alleys like a cloister surrounded by ranges of buildings with a keep at the SW. angle. On the E. wall of the latter is the string-course, once internal, above the high table of the first-floor hall which formed the southern range. Across the court is the chapel, also on the upper floor, with remains of interlaced arcading on both external and internal walls.[3] The plan at Sherborne explains Bishop Roger's contemporary castle at Old Sarum, where the 'Great Tower' has been identified as another courtyard house with a tower.[4] Little is left of Roger's stronghold at Devizes.[5] Unlike Bishop Roger, who died, disgraced by Stephen in 1139, Henry of Blois had the opportunity to rebuild his castle — like palaces dismantled by Henry II in 1155,[6] on his return from

[1] *Archaeological Journal*, XCII (1935), pp. 167–242.
[2] *Antiquaries Journal*, XLIV (1964), pp. 196–202; XLV (1965), pp. 243–9.
[3] *R.C.H.M. Dorset*, I (1952), pp. 64–66, pl. 90, 91, 210.
[4] *M.O.W.* guide (1961), pp. 5–9, plan.
[5] R. Allen Brown, H. M. Colvin and A. J. Taylor: *The History of the King's Works; the Middle Ages* (1963), pp. 626–8.
[6] The Pipe Roll of 1155 gives the cost of their demolition by the Sheriff of Hampshire, M. W. Thompson. *M.O.W.* guide (1961), pp. 6, 16–17, *Medieval Archaeology*, IV (1960), pp. 81–94, pls. XIV – XVIII.

exile in 1159. So there are two periods of twelfth-century work in most of his buildings. At Farnham Castle, within the shell keep, there was discovered in 1958 a great tower 45 ft. square, of c. 1138, which had been completely hidden and forgotten. In the domestic block SE. of his shell keep, the bishop's once-aisled hall may date from his first period of building, with later alterations to the doorways. The first-floor chapel could be c. 1140. Its floor is on ground level to the courtyard, where the blocked thirteenth-century arcade can be seen. At Bishop's Waltham the Ministry has consolidated the walls and revealed a chapel undercroft with central columns and apsidal end. This belongs to the early twelfth century, as does part of the S. curtain wall and an original internal gate-house. These represent the building of c. 1135 by Henry of Blois. But most of the Norman work seen today dates from the bishop's return from France in 1159 — probably before his death in 1171. We know that Henry II was received here in 1182. The new buildings were added on the outside of the old curtain walls, represented by the E. wall of the hall in the W. range and N. wall of the S. (great chamber) block. The hall was originally on the first floor, and at the S. end some faint remains of the arcading once behind the high table can be seen. Later the undercroft was filled in, and it became a ground-floor hall on a bank, with fine Perpendicular type windows of the late fourteenth or early fifteenth century. N. of the hall are two service rooms and kitchen, and S. of it a gallery and a tower at the angle with the S. range which contained the bishop's private rooms.[1]

At Winchester Martin Biddle's excavations for the Ministry show that Wolvesey Palace[2] was the largest and most elaborate Norman house. To the west hall built c. 1100 by his predecessor William Giffard,[3] Bishop Henry added a grand staircase with an entrance doorway, of which surviving ornament suggests a date of c. 1140. Across a courtyard he built the east hall (c. 1129–35), and c. 1135 the two halls were linked by a curtain wall forming the N. side of the

[1] *Medieval Archaeology*, I (1957), p. 154; II (1958), p. 194; V (1961), p. 317; VI–VII (1962–3), p. 319; VIII (1964), p. 248; IX (1965), p. 184. Royal Archaeological Institute, *Programme of the Summer Meeting at Southampton* (1966), pp. 50–1, fig. 15.

[2] *Antiquaries Journal*, XLIV (1964), pp. 212–15; XLV (1965), p. 260; XLVI (1966), pp. 327–8, XLVII (1967), pp. 272–6, XLVIII (1968), pp. 280–4; XLIX (1969), pp. 324–5; L (1970), pp. 323–5; LII (1972), pp. 125–31. *Medieval Archaeology*, VIII (1964), p. 248; IX (1965), p. 184; X (1966), pp. 184, 186; XI (1967), p. 282; XII (1968), p. 173; XIII (1969), p. 250; XIV (1970), pp. 172–3; XV (1971), p. 143.

[3] At Taunton Castle the works of both bishops can be found. Portions of Giffard's early twelfth-century hall remain, and its SW. end wall retains marks of two parallel barrel vaults, the hall above being probably wooden and aisled, perhaps like Bishop Roger's contemporary hall at Devizes. There was a similar vault set transversely under the adjoining solar, but its span was reduced in the thirteenth century by thickening the end (SW.) wall, blocking the inner portion of a loop window when a ground floor hall replaced the twelfth-century one. Henry of Blois built the keep. C. A. R. Radford and A. D. Hallam, *Somerset Archaeological & Natural History Proc.*, XCVIII (1953), pp. 55–96.

courtyard, and across the N. end of the west first-floor hall a new block was constructed so serve as a 'reredorter' to it. In 1138 a keep (*turris*) was added to part of the east wail of the great hall,[1] and about that time a parallel wall to the curtain was built on the courtyard side. Then, c. 1160, after the bishop's return from exile, a gatehouse was added on the outside of the original N. curtain, on the site of a chapel of the Saxon palace, and a new curtain parallel to the N. end of the east hall. This great hall of c. 1130 was originally of ground-floor type with low aisles, but the bishop in the latter years of his episcopate, c. 1159–71, transformed it into a first-floor one with a clerestory gallery. The decoration on the latter and the high table arcading, widely spaced ball ornament, shows the influence of Cluny, his old monastery, where he had spent his exile, 1155 – c. 1158. In the thirteenth century it became a ground-floor hall again, with a single western aisle, and the keep became the great kitchen. Particularly interesting was the find of a well house in the NW. corner of the courtyard, serving Bishop Giffard's west hall of c. 1100. Its original feed-pipe is a continuation of that below the east hall, so it must be c. 1130 or earlier, thus antedating the celebrated monastic water-works plan of 1165 for Canterbury.

But the greatest feudal building must have been the vast hall at Westminster, built for William Rufus in 1097–9 (239 ft. 6 in. by 67 ft. 6 in.). Its monumental quality was further emphasized in the late fourteenth century when Hugh Herland's new roof allowed the floor space to be cleared of probably timber posts sub-dividing the span. Possibly an arcade, like that of Hereford,[2] may be envisaged; however, the arcade is a feature not natural to wood, but influenced by stone construction. It was absent at Leicester and probably Farnham. At Westminster no evidence of post holes has yet been found, but it is known that the present floor is 3 ft. 9 in. higher than the Norman level; and in the repairs of c. 1925 evidence of the original window arrangement was discovered, built up in Yevele's remodelling (1394–1402), which altered the baying. There were twelve bays, each with a window on the side walls, these flanked by two minor round-headed arches giving access to a barrel-vaulted passage. The large window and passage arches were supported on piers formed by four grouped shafts having cushion capitals. Some carved examples of the latter are preserved.[3] Remains of red and blue paint, with black lines, found in the wall passages, give us an idea of the brilliant colour which must have embellished the hall. Thus the hall of the Red King, although on a grand scale, with stone walls, seems to have had its piers in wood, although the evidence is not conclusive. His great-nephew, Henry II, certainly had stone columns in the hall of his palace at Clarendon. The mortices of their

[1] The Annals of Winchester give this date, saying that in 1138 Bishop Henry of Blois 'fecit . . . aedificare domum quasi palatium cum turri fortissima in Wintonia'.

[2] See S. R. Jones and J. T. Smith, 'The great hall of the bishop's palace at Hereford', *Medieval Archaeology*, IV (1960), pp. 69–80.

[3] Exhibited in the Jewel Tower at Westminster.

bases have been excavated, and suggest shafts 2 ft. in diameter. The stone hall (83 ft. by 51 ft.) was of four bays, and had a dais at the upper end. It may date from the year 1176–7 when a very large sum (£268 17s 9d) was spent on the palace; also 2s 6d for bringing marble columns to Clarendon. Some idea of its appearance may be obtained from the smaller but very elaborate castle hall which remains at Oakham (66 ft. by 44 ft.), also of four bays, and dated by its ornament to c. 1190. The stone columns, again 2 ft. in diameter, have magnificent Corinthianesque capitals below arches enriched with dog-tooth ornament, which could have supported a clerestory wall, originally rising clear of the aisles.[1]

One of the most complete Norman houses left to us is Christchurch Castle Hall. It is now cleared of ivy, and carefully treated by the Ministry of Works who received guardianship in 1946. One oblong stone compartment on each floor is left, but there is evidence of a wooden sub-division. While the entrance is usually near the end of the hall, here it is a third of the way from the end of the block. It seems to have opened into a transverse passage between wooden partitions, long since perished, through which doors would have opened northwards into the hall and southwards into the solar or private apartments. Here the solar was at the lower end of the hall, the high table with a specially elaborate window behind it being at the north.

But it is not by official bodies alone that Norman houses have been preserved. At Hemingford Grey Mrs. L. M. Boston made a complete restoration of the Manor House in 1939–40, unblocking more of the twelfth-century hall windows, no longer divided by an attic floor, and opening out the fireplace between its sturdy jamb-shafts with scalloped capitals and restoring its segmental head.[2] Other houses saved include Luddesdown Court in Kent and Saltford Manor House in Somerset, although at the latter the later chapel had collapsed before the rescue of the house by Mr. A. R. Beauchamp after 1945. The fine twelfth-century window is no longer divided by a floor, and shows an inner order with roll-moulded arch supported by shafts with cushion capitals like those outside, and similar ones to the chevron and lozenge-ornamented rear arch. It is reminiscent of the N. and S. windows of West Malling c. 1140–50 which have chevron-decorated rear arches, here segmental, supported by fluted imposts to roll-shafts with steep moulded bases. A solar window retains its window seats, and thirteenth-century wall-paintings of a Madonna and Child and a wheel of fortune have been uncovered.

Merton Hall (the School of Pythagoras) c. 1200, was surveyed by the Royal Commission on Historical Monuments.[3] A long domestic block was originally sub-divided, here by a timber partition, between hall and solar. Contemporary with this range and opening out of the

[1] C. A. R. Radford, *Archaeological Journal*, CXII (1955), p. 183. J. T. Smith finds no clerestory evidence in surviving aisled halls. At Oakham he believes the original roof was heightened with re-used Norman masonry in the seventeenth-century alterations, *Medieval Archaeology*, IV (1960), p. 76.

[2] L. M. Boston, *Memory in a House* (1973); P. G. M. Dickinson, *Historic Hemingford Grey* (1946), pp. 28–34.

[3] *Cambridge*, II (1959), pp. 377–9.

upper 'solar' part, making an L-plan, is a short northern wing, later extended, called the 'solar wing' in a deed of 1270. We have thus an early building with two solars.

More research work has been done, particularly by Mr. P. A. Faulkner, on early medieval houses.[1] At Southampton he considers that 'Canute's Palace' (the Long House) contains an upper hall-house, similar in size and plan to Christchurch Castle hall, with an eastern extension which may have been a warehouse. The area has been excavated under the direction of Mr. J. Pallister and the Southampton City Museums Department. For 'King John's House', he suggests that the whole N. half was a first-floor hall, divided by a wall, at least partially arcaded, from two chambers to the south. Below the western half was a warehouse with arches once open to the quay, with two rooms behind. In the blocking of the one original round-headed arch and its segmental thirteenth-century neighbour were set what the late B. St. J. O'Neil considered the earliest cannon loops, dating from after the French sacking of Southampton in 1337.

Since 1935 more light on the Norman houses also has been thrown by documentary evidence, particularly by the researches of Sir Francis Hill whose *Mediaeval Lincoln* was published in 1948. He has discovered that in the late twelfth century the fashionable quarter for rich merchants was the suburb of Wigford, south of the city, which is now incorporated with it. It is therefore not surprising that here should be found St. Mary's Guildhall, the headquarters of what must have been an important social-religious guild. It was named after Our Lady, patron saint of Lincoln, and its chapel seems to have been the church of St. Andrew, which stood nearly opposite. In the next century Henry III was a brother of 'the ancient guild of St. Mary', and in 1389 an important citizen, Ralf de Scremby, is styled 'master and warden of the old great gild in honour of God and St. Mary'. St. Mary's Guild was built, according to stylistic evidence, c. 1180–90, and its entrance range with great archway remains, an elaborate string-course, and a beautiful capital at the dais end of the hall which was once above one wing of the courtyard, is left, partly rebuilt. Even now there is a certain magnificence about it, and it must have been sumptuous in its prime. The homes of the great merchants were built around. Next to it was the house where Adam the first mayor of Lincoln lived. He was the alderman of the guild merchant from c. 1185, and mayor in 1210. Neighbours of his in Wigford were Godwin and Reimbald, both called 'the Rich', and on the long list of those fined for assaulting the Jews in 1191.

Very few of these early merchant houses have survived. But there is documentary evidence that they were in stone, mentioned thus in the records, as this was remarkable in days when ordinary people

[1] 'Domestic Planning from the Twelfth to the Fourteenth Centuries', *Archaeological Journal*, CXV (1958), pp. 150–83, plans. 'Medieval Undercrofts and Town Houses', ibid., CXXIII (1966), pp. 120–35.

were content with wooden buildings; and also a landmark. Near the Jewish houses in Canterbury, Dr. Urry has found references to the 'stone house of Goldwin the Mercer' and others. The stone vaults remaining at Canterbury must have been the basements of such buildings; also that in 24 St. Thomas Street in Winchester.

In Lincoln, where stone was the local building material, there would be many more; and indeed numbers were left as late as the eighteenth century. The observant Mr. King remarked in 1782 on a 'circumstance most peculiar to it of all cities in England; which is the vast number of beautiful Saxon and Norman doorways, constructed in the most finished manner, and to be met with in every part of the streets, and in the walls of what are now the most private houses'.[1] But Defoe attributed this wealth of 'Gothic remains' to civic decay.[2]

The Jews occupied a special position in the early medieval economy. Unable to take part in the usual crafts of the time, being prevented through religious reasons from taking the guild oath to the Trinity, they concentrated on finance and thus filled a definite need in times when no Christian was permitted by canon law to lend money on interest. Indeed they had control of a large proportion of the actual coin of the country in days when so much capital was locked up in land. Barter was of no avail when great projects were on hand, and the Jews provided the funds for such enterprises as the equipment of armies or the building of cathedrals and monasteries. The most famous of them was Aaron of Lincoln, who flourished from 1166–85, and at his death had no less than one king (of Scotland), five earls, one archbishop, two bishops, nine Cistercian abbeys (including Rievaulx) and the towns of Winchester and Southampton, besides many smaller debtors, on his books. These are recorded on the Pipe Rolls, as his property went to the Crown in 1185. The Abbey of St. Albans owed him much: its chronicler relates how 'Aaron the Jew who held us in his debt coming to the house of St. Alban in great pride and boasting, with threats kept on boasting that it was he who made the window for our St. Alban, and that he had prepared for the saint a home when he was without one'.[3] One bishop of Lincoln (Chesney, 1148–66) pawned the ornaments of his church, which were only redeemed from Aaron by his successor.[4] Aaron had agents throughout the country, and owned a house in London, in Lothbury near Walbrook, but Lincoln was apparently his headquarters. However, the so-called Aaron's House there, alike in date and build to Jew's House and probably with a similar twelfth-century occupant, was *not* owned by him. He lived in Lincoln c. 1166–85 but in another part of the city, namely the Bail. Aaron was a great source of revenue to Henry II from taxation during his lifetime and at his death, when the Exchequer set up a special department, the *Scaccarium Aaronis*, to collect the debts due to him. In their stone houses Jewish financiers kept not only gold

[1] *Archaeologia*, VI (1782), p. 261.

[2] *Tour through the Whole Island Of Great Britain* (1724–6), Everyman's Library edition, II, p. 91.

[3] *Gesta Sancti Albani*, ed. H. T. Riley, Rolls Series (1867–9), p. 193.

[4] J. W. F. Hill: *Mediaeval Lincoln* (1948), p. 218.

and silver, like a bank, but also the deeds relative to their loans, hence the need for a very strong fireproof building.

Another important Jewish financier, Jacob, is associated with Canterbury. He contributed nearly half the city's grant, in 1194, towards the ransom of Richard I, and seems to have been the wealthiest of a colony of Jews who appear in the city c. 1180. Here we know exactly where he lived from documentary evidence, and the County Hotel preserves in its cellar (and above ground until 1927) a very thick wall of the 'great stone house' which he built just before 1200.[1] The front part of the hotel covers the three plots of land which he bought for this purpose, and behind, with its frontage to Stour Street, earlier called 'Heathen Man's Lane' was the Synagogue, while the house of another Jew, Benedict or Baruch, lay beyond. In Norwich, the late twelfth-century 'Music House'[2] with its vaulted cellars, may have been the residence of the great financier, Isaac the Jew. He is portrayed in a thirteenth-century cartoon in the Public Record Office as a three-faced king of Norwich; he died in 1199, his property passing to King John. From a resemblance in architectural detail to the Priory Infirmary, the house is believed to date from c. 1175, and thus probably built by Isaac himself, though his father (Abraham) and grandfather (Moses) seem to have had an earlier house in Conisford on this site, or nearby.

[1] *The House of Jacob the Jew of Canterbury* (1953), based on research by Dr. W. Urry, contains translations of the documents of 1190 and site plans.

[2] E. A. Kent, *Norfolk Archaeology*, XXVIII (1945), pp. 28–38; W. Buston, *Country Life* (Aug. 21, 1942), pp. 360–1.

INTRODUCTION

Norman domestic architecture in England has been neglected in the past. Indeed this has been, until recently, the fate of the medieval dwelling-house in general. Even now there are less than half a dozen books on that subject, headed by the work of Turner and Parker,[1] to whom credit as pioneers is due.

The reason is, of course, to be found in a scarcity of recognisable examples, occasioned by the very nature of the dwelling-house, more liable to alteration and destruction than any other type of architecture. Norman houses, being earliest, have naturally suffered most ; indeed their only chance of escape lay in a greater sturdiness of wall which is sometimes the sole means of recognition. Hence there is even a general ignorance that twelfth-century buildings existed other than those of an ecclesiastical or military character ; the Normans were associated with warfare or piety, and housed accordingly in castle or monastery. Thus in some works on domestic architecture, 'keeps' form the illustrations for the twelfth century, and the reader can even assume that subsequent houses were developed from these. When the author is aware of Romanesque houses—and then it is usually Jew's House, Lincoln, and Boothby Pagnell manor that are known—they are mentioned rather as anomalies.

This may account for the attribution of a Jewish origin to certain houses, all in towns, which indeed derive a local fame from that assumption.[2] For if the Normans lived in castles, then the Jews must be

[1] The first volume of a series mostly is by Parker (*Domestic Architecture of the Middle Ages*). Some confusion arises because in this the twelfth and thirteenth century volume (1851), Turner is given as the author, Parker the publisher. Turner apparently wrote the historical part, Parker the architectural. Turner died after the first volume was completed, and Parker continued the series. To avoid confusion the first volume is here referred to as 'Turner and Parker.'

[2] Jew's House, Jew's Court, Aaron the Jew's House, Lincoln ; Moyse's Hall, Bury St. Edmunds.

responsible for dwelling-houses. If not, King John may be chosen as the builder, for some reason not obvious unless as another example of his infamy.[1] But his name is commoner, and with greater reason, for houses of the thirteenth century,[2] these being, somewhat curiously, seldom ascribed to Jews.

There may be, however, some truth in the 'Jewish theory,' and notably with regard to the two houses at Lincoln assigned by tradition to such owners.[3] The Jews were accustomed to a higher standard of living than that of their simpler neighbours, many of whom, as in London,[4] were probably content with timber, wattle-and-daub, and the danger of fire. The Jews were rich, and had more to lose in a fire, also they were unpopular as money-lenders and so liable to attack by the mob. A stone house was thus preferred for reasons of comfort and protection. On the other hand, Lincoln, situated on the limestone belt, would be more likely to possess stone houses than London, to which any building-stone would have to be imported. Thus such houses remaining in Lincoln need not be Jewish save by coincidence—and without proof it is only possible to state a long tradition, and to suggest that the rich decoration at Jew's House points to an owner of no small wealth,[5] and that the strength of the house is another argument in favour of a theory which is not unworthy of consideration.

However, it does not seem to apply in the case of Moyse's Hall. This building certainly occurs within the period before the Jews at St. Edmundsbury were expelled;[6] the name may be Jewish and is certainly old—it first occurs in a document of 1328. But the house may have become Jewish on the analogy of the

[1] Canute is a variant in Southampton, where King John already had one house.

[2] King John's Palace, Clipstone (Edwinstowe, Notts); King John's House, Warnford (Hants); Romsey (Hants); Tollard Royal (Wilts).

[3] Jew's Court is more doubtful, and not even certainly twelfth-century.

[4] Yet even in London the Jews had houses of stone, for in 1215 'the Barons . . . repaired the walles and gates of the Citie, with stones taken from the Jewe's broken houses,' Stow, *Survey of London* (Kingsford, 1908), i, 9 (also 30, 38, 280, 283).

[5] But similar, even richer decoration occurs at St. Mary's Guild, traditionally not Jewish but belonging to some guild, possibly one of masons. In the latter case, Jew's House may have been worked by members of it.

[6] 1190.

Lincoln examples, and possibly belonged to the monastery; we know that Abbot Samson (1182–1212) bought and erected stone houses in the borough, but unfortunately there is no proof that Moyse's Hall was one of them, though again it fits with regard to date. To sum up:—probably the Jews had stone houses for reasons of defence, wealth and importance, but it is unwise to consider that every surviving Norman house necessarily had a Jewish owner.

There were other people of wealth in the twelfth-century besides Jew and baron: that is, persons who could afford to build a substantial house, and especially in districts where stone was abundant. This statement would apply chiefly to the towns; in country places the view is probably correct that surviving Norman houses were manor houses, the dwellings of knights, or granges on the estates of richer nobles who had castle halls elsewhere. But in the towns the craft and merchant guilds were increasingly active in the twelfth century, and it may be that guild-houses frequently existed like the building at Lincoln traditionally assigned to St. Mary's Guild, the nature of which is obscure. There were also well-to-do merchants in thriving places like Southampton, one of the chief ports of England, where the so-called King John's House suggests such an owner in its arrangement. The question of defence concerned these less than it did the Jew, but they also had valuable stores to protect from fire and theft, and money to build a stone basement for that purpose, with a pleasant hall above to live in. The twelfth century has too long been relegated to lord and villein; and the attribution of wealth alone to the noble and the money-lending classes has caused misconceptions apparent in theories concerning the origin of the Norman house.

THEORIES OF ORIGIN

The 'castle origin' of the English house has now been abandoned by responsible archaeologists. The keep was certainly used in many cases continuously for domestic purposes, especially in the first half of the twelfth century, as at Norwich,[1] London,[2] and Canterbury,[3] and it became a special type of stone house which belongs to military rather than to domestic architecture. Towards the end of the twelfth century, however, when stone curtain-walls replaced the timber palisade, the keep was found to be unnecessary, and a return was made to the unfortified type of house in the bailey, which was less restricted as to space, and which had probably constituted the hall in many twelfth-century castles.[4]

Contemporary existence, with the keep, of the house in the bailey would appear to disprove the theory of 'castle origin.' Nor is it likely that the dwelling-house originated even there, protected by an outer line of walls. Its incorporation in the castle is typologically later than its use as a separate entity, although this cannot be proved chronologically by the examples surviving, Scolland's Hall at Richmond Castle antedating all the other houses except the doubtful type at Nytimber.

A similar argument occurs with regard to the theory that the dwelling-house had a monastic origin. It is urged that monks being more advanced in building, part of their plan was taken and adapted for ordinary domestic use, and that the 'frater' and its adjoining passage and warming chamber served as pattern for the hall, screens and offices of the medieval house. But in the twelfth century the refectory occurred both on ground and first floor according to the level of the site, while the hall was as a rule on the first floor, and screens have by no means been proved the rule in the Romanesque house. Perhaps stronger, however, is the argument of typology. To make the dwelling-house posterior to its use in a specialised group of buildings is to put the effect before the cause.

[1] H. Braun, *The English Castle* (Batsford, 1936), pp. 33–34.

[2] *Ibid*, p. 32. A great hall was also provided apart from the White Tower.

[3] *Ibid*, p. 35.

[4] Eleventh and twelfth century halls of this kind occur at Richmond, Chepstow, and traces at Ludlow, Newark and Porchester. See Hamilton Thompson, *Military Architecture in England during the Middle Ages* (1912), pp. 55–56, 107, 188 *et seq.*

The primitive ancestors of the English house need not here be considered. The question has been fully discussed in several works on domestic architecture,[1] and in any case concerns rather the derivation of the medieval timber house, of which no known examples remain of the twelfth century beyond fragments of arcading in certain once-aisled halls. In view of the latter, however, it will be interesting to examine the possibility of a Saxon origin to the Norman house.

It is doubtful whether any Romanesque stone house dates to the pre-Conquest period, although several examples have been claimed as such,[2] largely owing to the presence in them of herring-bone walling, now known to be generally of early Norman and not Saxon date. Thus, unless definite proof arises to the contrary, it may be assumed that the Saxons used stone only for sacred structures, and not always for these, while for domestic use they were content to follow the Nordic tradition of building in wood. As the late Mr. Nathaniel Lloyd has shown, 'timber' and 'timbrung' are Old English words for a building.

Unfortunately wood does not endure save in exceptional circumstances,[3] and there is only one example remaining of a timber pre-Conquest building. This is the nave of Greenstead church in Essex,[4] which indicates that in the late Saxon period one type of walling consisted in uprights of split logs, partially resembling Swiss chalets or huts in the Rockies.[5] It was an extravagant use of wood in a country of luxuriant forests, and in contrast with the more economical and scientific method seen in the later medieval half-timber houses, where wattle and daub were used as filling for a wooden framework.

Apart from this survivor, there is no direct evidence

[1] N. Lloyd, p. 7 *et seq.* S. O. Addy, *Evolution of the English House* (1935), pp. 1–92.

[2] Barton or Manor Farm, Nytimber, Sussex. Early hall at Chilham Castle, Kent. Luddesdown Court, near Cobham, Kent. In the latter there is no herring-bone masonry but triangular-headed openings are claimed to have existed.

[3] The peat-finds of Scandinavia, especially the Gokstad and Oseberg ships (in 1880 and 1903). See R. W. Chambers, *Beowulf, An Introduction* (1932), p. 363.

[4] *R.C.H.M. Essex* ii, 112. Photograph in Lloyd, p. 7.

[5] But in these the logs are laid horizontally.

as to the construction of Saxon halls. The student is forced to look for material in contemporary manuscripts and in probable descendants.

Illustrations in manuscripts are sometimes untrustworthy, for it should be remembered that the artist was conservative and bound by a drawing tradition not always native to him; thus the houses he depicts may be of types standardised elsewhere.[1] Descriptions in writing are probably more reliable, and recent scholarship has shown that the epic 'Beowulf,' although its characters are Scandinavian, gives in its atmosphere an impression of seventh- and eighth-century Northumbria.[2]

Other evidence is obtainable from probable survivals of an old building tradition, and Mr. Clapham has suggested that certain features in medieval barns and aisled halls indicate a remote half-barbaric origin to the type.[3] Descendants of early Germanic halls are also to be found in the original homes of the Saxons, in Friesland and elsewhere, for here modern houses are still built in the ancient manner, often sheltering men and cattle under the same roof.[4]

From such sources we can obtain some idea of what the Saxon hall was like. It was a timber building containing a single apartment at ground level. In 'Beowulf' the great 'mead hall' (medoheal), is described further as having lofty gables, golden in colour, timber walls strengthened with bands of iron.[5] The hall was probably aisled or barnlike in construction, although no definite mention is made of this in the epic. No doubt such a method would be used for wide halls, but not for smaller buildings such as bowers or private bed-chambers, which with the hall were enclosed by a single homestead hedge or bank. The present church of Sta. Maria de Naranco in Northern Spain is said to be the only surviving example of a

[1] See N. Lloyd, p. 3 *et seq.*

[2] 'Beowulf' was probably written c. 730, but the earliest manuscript dates c. 1000.

[3] Clapham and Godfrey, *Some Famous Buildings and their Story*, p. 67 *et seq.*

[4] Lloyd, p. 5.

[5] Beowulf, lines 82, 166–7, 484–5, 773–5, 998. See also discussion in R.W. Chambers, *Beowulf, An Introduction*, pp. 361–2.

Germanic hall.[1] This is, however, a stone building, but apparently on a similar plan to the wooden ones. It is an aisled hall with curious piers reminiscent of timber construction, and crowned with cubiform capitals. The aisles, however, have gone, and the nave arches have been blocked. At each end is a triple arcade, similar to the chancel arrangement of the seventh-century Kentish churches built by Italianate craftsmen. The piers of these arches, however, in the Spanish hall, are grooved for doors, and the arrangement thus fits in with the famous description in Bede, where the hall had an entrance in each of the end walls, through which the sparrow flew symbolical of the life of man.[2] In contrast with the usual medieval plan of upper end and dais, the principal seats here, and apparently in 'Beowulf,' would be in the middle of the hall, facing the 'high seat pillars' and the central hearth.

This is in essence the same type as the aisled halls of the twelfth century and later. Mr. Lloyd even believed that it is a Saxon form in contradistinction to the Norman type of compact first-floor hall.[3] There may be some truth in this,[4] but on the other hand the Germanic type was just as likely in Normandy for large halls constructed in wood. Certainly there is no real evidence that the first-floor hall occurred in pre-Conquest England, but that is to be expected as it is essentially a stone type of building. However, there is one isolated suggestion that such was the case. In the Anglo-Saxon Chronicle for the year 978, we read how the Council was held in an upper chamber, the floor of which apparently collapsed, projecting the Witan into the room below, all save the holy Dunstan who 'alone stood upon a beam.' Another instance,

[1] Albrecht Haupt, *Die älteste Kunst, insbesondere die Baukunst der Germanen, von der Völkwanderung bis zu Karl dem Grossen* (Leipsig, 1909), p. 208.

[2] Bede, *Historia Ecclesiastica*, Book II, chap. xiii. (C. Plummer: *Baedæ Opera Historica*, i, 112).

[3] Lloyd, p. 17. He also notes (p. 174) that the French tradition lingered on in Scotland where many houses in the sixteenth century had their living-rooms at first-floor level.

[4] William of Malmesbury criticises the Saxons for their drinking habits and poor dwellings ; he contrasts the Normans who drank less and built better. *Gesta Regum Anglorum*, Book III, §245 (ed. T. D. Hardy, 1840, vol. ii, 418).

more explainable, is given in the Bayeux ' tapestry ' where Harold's ' Aula ' at Bosham is depicted as a hall over a vaulted basement.[1] But this is natural as the embroidery was worked by Normans who had probably never seen a Saxon house, and pictured the kind to which they were accustomed.[2]

From the evidence available we can say that the aisled hall certainly had analogies in the Saxon period. The same would apply to the simple type of unaisled ground-floor hall, equally adapted to timber construction. But as we shall see later, the first-floor hall is a type unsuited to a wooden house, and probably only came in when stone began to be used for domestic buildings, that is, in England, in the late eleventh but especially the twelfth century.

DISTRIBUTION[3]

At present we know of 39 extant examples of Norman Domestic Architecture, but it must be remembered that most survivors are fragmentary or mutilated.

This includes 16 first-floor halls, of which 6 are town houses, 6 manor houses, and 4 occur in castles. Six aisled halls remain of twelfth-century date and 4 ground-floor halls without aisles. Besides these are the remains of 2 Bishop's Palaces, and the foundations of a royal one, 3 houses in which the sub-vaults alone are extant,[4] 4 examples of uncertain type, and 3 of doubtful date. This does not include documentary evidence of houses now destroyed, such as the small house in Blue Anchor Lane, Southampton, the London sub-vaults at Corbet Court and Southwark, and the hall of Devizes Castle.

It is curious to note that so many examples occur in towns, where the scarcity of building-land would lead to more changes than are normal in country districts.[5] As it is, Lincoln and Southampton furnish

[1] For illustration see Baldwin Brown, *The Life of Saxon England in its relation to the Arts* (1903), p. 104.

[2] N. Lloyd, p. 174. Normandy, not England, is its accepted place of origin.

[3] See classified list of houses.

[4] Or retain original features, in the case of the Redmarley example.

[5] But in towns stone-work was encouraged to prevent the spread of fire.

the most notable houses, and with the exception of Oakham and Boothby Pagnell, the most unaltered.

Stone is the chief building material to survive ; so naturally most examples occur in the rich limestone belt which crosses England from north-east to south-west. West of this is the sandstone country, where, however, half-timber seems to have been preferred for houses throughout the later Middle Ages. No doubt this was also true of the twelfth century, and may account for the few Norman houses of sandstone that are known. More, however, may come to light. East of the belt lie the great areas of chalk and clay, a country poor in building-stone. Notwithstanding, several Romanesque houses occur in the south-east ; in fact it is Sussex and Kent, after Hampshire and Lincoln, which contribute the most examples. If a line is drawn from Humber to Bristol Channel it is the south-eastern half of England that preserves most Norman houses.

BERKSHIRE : APPLETON MANOR. (Plates i A, xi A, Fig. 1.)

Appleton is a village 6 miles SW. of Oxford and the manor-house lies S. of the church. It was built c. 1210,[1] but is here included as an example of the Transition, not only in style but in house development. The former is visible in the elaborate N. entrance, an opening of three orders with jamb shafts, for this has the Norman round arch together with the deep rolls, circular abaci, and stiff-stalk capitals of the Early English period. The latter is seen in the relationship of this doorway, in the normal twelfth-century position for the entrance, with two others in the wall at right angles to it. These lead to the offices and are individually of some interest, having roll hoods with upturned ends and a flatly carved head ornament between, but their importance to us lies in their position. With the entrance they fit exactly into the normal medieval scheme, and but for the absence of ' screens ' possibly supplanted by a Tudor partition containing fireplaces, we have an entry typical of all the Middle Ages except the twelfth century. There was originally another doorway opposite the entrance in the position now occupied by a modern window. But for these three doorways there are no original features ; the hall is now divided into two storeys and the exterior has been refaced. Norman roll-mouldings are re-used on the NW. angle, and on the jambs of the Tudor fireplace. There are traces of a later medieval newel stair in the E. wall, and a sixteenth-century porch protects the Norman entrance. A dry moat surrounds the house on three sides.

[1] The dating is on stylistic grounds throughout.

Condition : Good as far as the doorways are concerned, although some of the entrance shafts are gone, and the bases corroded.

References : *Country Life* (May 11, 1929), pp. 670–677. Good photographs, dated plan with no scale.
V.C.H.[1] *Berks*, iv (1914, published 1924), p. 335.
Turner and Parker, p. 29.
Berks, Bucks and Oxon Arch. Journal xxiii (1917), no. 2, figs. 35, 36.
D. and S. Lyson : *Magna Britannia I* (1806), pp. 212, 234 (Drawing).

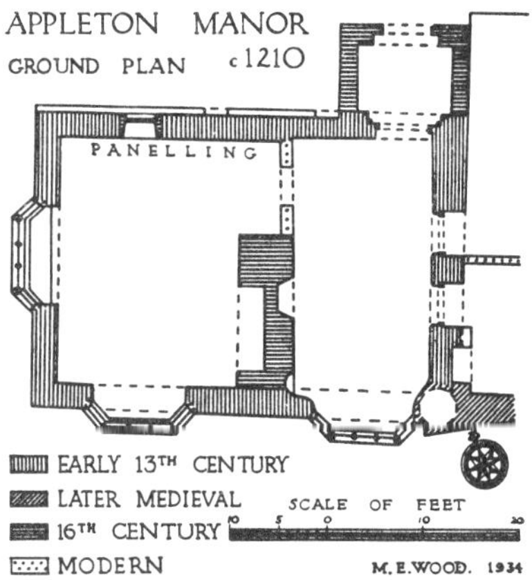

FIG. 1.

BERKSHIRE : SUTTON COURTENAY—'NORMAN HALL.' (Plate 1 B, Fig. 2.)

'Norman Hall' stands opposite the church, and was built c. 1190. The walls are 2 ft. 8 in. in thickness, of random rubble, with ashlar quoins, in the NE. of which are two curious oblong mortise-holes, 10 in. by 3 in., c. 7 ft. up from the ground. Original features comprise two doorways to N. and S., and seven lancets, only three being unblocked. The S. doorway is the more elaborate having rolls, nail-head and dog-tooth ornament in the arch, and originally jamb-shafts, of which foliated capitals remain. The N. doorway is of one order only, with roll-shafts and slight capitals. The windows are high in the walls, as in monastic refectories. Additions include an ancient queen-post roof, and a fifteenth-century E. window.

[1] *Common Abbreviations :* V.C.H. = Victoria County History. R.C.H.M. = Royal Commission on Historical Monuments. Arch. Journal= Archaeological Journal.

This is interesting as an example of the unaisled ground-floor hall, but some authorities believe it to be a chapel.[1] It is rightly orientated and the N. and S. doorways almost face towards the W. angles of the building. A further suggestion has been made that the chapel belonged to a grange of the Abbey of Abingdon.[2] But there is no documentary evidence that such a grange existed at Sutton Courtenay, only a farm owned by the Abbey,[3] and otherwise there seems no reason for a chapel within a few yards of a church of contemporary date.

'Norman Hall' is a recent title for the building, but it may be justified by an absence of windows on the W. half of the N. wall, which suggests an original annexe on the site of part of the modern range, and thus a domestic type of plan. However, these windows

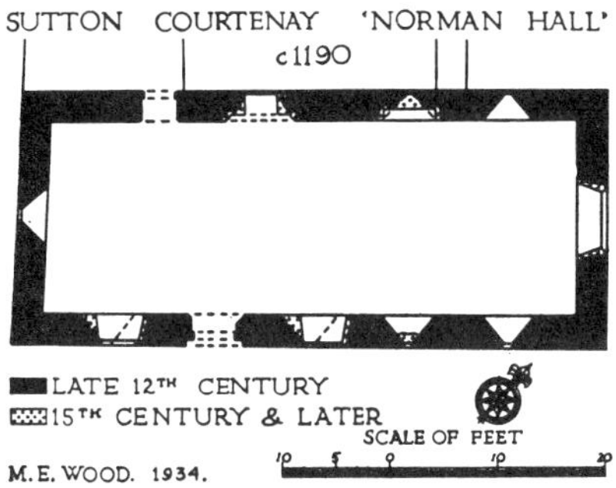

FIG. 2.

may have been blocked when the modern wing was built, and the Tudor fireplace was recently inserted. But if so, it is strange that they are invisible, as some of the other lancets, though blocked, can still be traced. Mr. A. E. Preston is probably right in his belief that the present building represents the hall built by Reginald de Courtenay about 1190, possibly on the site of a residence of the first Norman Kings.

Condition : Good.

References : *V.C.H. Berks* iv (1914, pub. 1924), p. 371.
Arch. Journal LXVII (1910), p. 375.
Berks, Bucks and Oxon Arch. Journal xi (1905), p. 113 (C. Lynam), drawings and plan (¼ in. scale); xxv, no. 1 (1919), pp. 23–38 (A. E. Preston); xxv, no. 2 (1920), pp. 94–113 (A. E. Preston).
Newbury and District Field Club vi (1895–1911), p. 81 (C. E. Keyser), Pl. xix (S. Doorway).

[1] Mr. C. Lynam, the late Sir William Hope and Sir H. Brakspear. V.C.H. says 'not improbable.'

[2] The late Mr. C. E. Keyser in *Newbury and District Field Club.*

[3] Mr. A. E. Preston in *Berks, Bucks and Oxon Arch. Journal*, xxv, no. 2 (1920), p. 96.

CAMBRIDGESHIRE: CAMBRIDGE—MERTON HALL (School of Pythagoras, or the Stone House).

Merton Hall is situated in Northampton Street and comprises a Norman house built c. 1200, a thirteenth-century solar, fourteenth-century buttresses, and a sixteenth-century wing. The Norman portion is a mutilated first-floor hall built of clunch, and the principal features are two damaged windows of two lights, with internal jamb-shafts; the once elaborately vaulted basement is now hardly recognisable as such.

Reference: J. M. Gray: *The School of Pythagoras, Cambridge* (Camb. Antiq. Soc., quarto, pub. N.S. iv, 1932). This contains recent plan and photographs, also eighteenth-century views, and the plan and section by Richard West (1739).
Turner and Parker, p. 53.

DEVONSHIRE: EXETER—HOUSE IN PRESTON STREET.

A building at the junction of Preston and King Streets has portions of mid twelfth-century walls interspersed with fifteenth-century work, also part of a Norman doorway with chevron, lozenge and pellets in the arch.

Condition: A casualty of the 1944 bombing; since demolished.

Reference: *Devon and Cornwall Notes and Queries* viii (1914–15), part i, p. 161 (E. K. Prideaux), plan and photographs.

DORSET: SHERBORNE CASTLE.

This was a palace of Bishop Roger of Sarum (1101–1139). It is built of Ham Hill oolite, and important as a large house of the twelfth century, including a hall, keep, and other buildings round a courtyard, also a gateway in the outer walls. A good chevron one-light window remains in the first floor of the N. range, also interlaced arcading on the S. external wall. There are loop-windows and part of a barrel vault in the E. wing, and the keep has a massive subvault and central pier with scallop capital.

Condition: Preservative works in progress.

Reference: *Arch. Journal* LXXXVII (1930), pp. 422–7. Description by Brakspear. S. Toy's plans of the site (undated) and keep (dated).

DURHAM: DURHAM CASTLE—PUDSEY'S HALL INCLUDING CONSTABLE'S HALL OR NORMAN GALLERY.

Pudsey's Hall forms the N. front of the castle, and dates c. 1170. There is a magnificent entrance doorway to the first-floor hall, consisting of three large and two smaller orders enriched with double billet, lozenge and other ornament; and an elaborate system of chevron wall-arcading associated with the windows to S. and W.

References : *V.C.H.* iii (1928), pp. 64–91, with dated plan ($\frac{1}{32}$ in. scale).
A. Hamilton Thompson, *Military Architecture in England during the Middle Ages* (1912), pp. 198–202, with illustrations, including a good drawing of the entrance.

GLOUCESTERSHIRE : HORTON COURT.

The W. wing is the Norman hall, dating c. 1140. Original features include a N. and S. doorway with chevron ornament and jamb-shafts, and two one-light windows on the N. wall. It is interesting as an aisleless ground-floor hall, and was probably the prebendal manor-house.

References : *Arch. Journal* LXXXVII (1930), pp. 449–451. Dated plan ($\frac{1}{24}$ in. scale) and illustration of S. wall.
Memorials of Gloucestershire (ed. Ditchfield, 1911), p. 133. C. E. Keyser. Illustration of N. door, p. 126, (the same article is contained in *Bristol and Glos. Arch. Soc. Trans.* xxi, p. 13).
W. J. Robinson, *West Country Manors* (1930), includes an article on Horton.

GLOUCESTERSHIRE : BRISTOL—LAW LIBRARY.

A late Norman hall is incorporated into the Law Library, Assize Courts, Small Street. Original features consist in two scalloped piers and a corbel supporting a pointed arcade. All is very much restored.

Reference : Notes in—
Clifton Antiq. Club, Proc. i (1888), p. 280–1.
Arch. Journal XXIII (1866), p. 150.

HAMPSHIRE : WINCHESTER—ST. THOMAS STREET SUBVAULT.

A twelfth-century subvault is contained in 24, St. Thomas Street. It consists of two bays of groined vaulting, with a dividing band supported on responds.

Reference : *V.C.H. Hants* v (1912), pp. 8, 9, plan and drawings.

HAMPSHIRE : WINCHESTER—WOLVESEY CASTLE (OR PALACE).

Wolvesey Castle lies S.E. of the Cathedral. Of the great hall, which concerns us most, only the N. and S. walls remain standing, but indicate an apartment of great length. It was built c. 1170 by Henry of Blois, Bishop of Winchester, but most of the magnificent ashlar has been peeled off for later buildings, leaving a rubble core of flint everywhere apparent. The N. wall contains, at first-floor level, fragments of arcading, five slightly pointed arches with pellet in triangle ornament, also a head-corbel, possibly cut later. On the S. wall a first-floor doorway opens into a passage communicating with the SW. tower, while other passages once occurred in the thickness of the N. wall at the level of the clerestory windows.

Condition : What remains of the hall is very much restored.

References : *V.C.H. Hants* v (1912), pp. 4, 13–14. Photograph before restoration.
Hants Field Club iii (1894–7), p. 207. Account of the castle and excavations in it by N. C. Nisbett, with plan and photograph.
(*Memorials of old Hampshire* (1906), pp. 204, 212, also contains Nisbett's article.)
Arch. Journal LXXXI (1924), p. 349 (Nisbett's plan).
F. Grose, *Antiquities of England and Wales* v (1777), p. 102, print.

HAMPSHIRE : BISHOP'S WALTHAM PALACE. (Plate iv B.)

The palace is an imposing ruin in the village of Bishop's Waltham, 9½ miles SE. of Winchester. It was originally built by Henry of Blois, Bishop of Winchester (1129–1171), but much that remains belongs to the fifteenth century. From eighteenth-century accounts the palace seems to have consisted of an outer and inner courtyard, but that arrangement is not now discernable owing to the fact that the W. range is practically all that exists above ground. From the modern road the great hall is visible with five fifteenth-century windows in the W. wall ; the opposite long wall has fallen. To the N. is a connecting block possibly containing the offices, and to the S. a more impressive survival in the form of a SW. tower of three storeys flanked by rooms to N. and E. This portion contains the twelfth-century features that remain, round-headed blocked or altered openings, and there is also a Transitional wall arcade just traceable on the S. wall of the hall. A later medieval barn stands on the E. side of the enclosure, and there is a ruined gateway near the N.W. corner of the site, also sixteenth-century brick towers overlooking a moat.

Condition : Ruinous and overgrown[1] but still impressive. It deserves more notice than it has received, and a detailed study will only follow after clearance and excavation.

References : *V.C.H. Hants* iii (1908), pp. 277–8. Illustration.
Arch. Journal LXXXI (1924), pp. 356–7.
F. Grose, *Antiquities of England and Wales* ii (1774), no page number, but see Hants, two prints of 1761.

HAMPSHIRE : SOUTHAMPTON—CANUTE'S PALACE. (Plate x B.)

The so-called ' Canute's Palace ' is situated in Porter Lane near the S. Quay. It is now a garage, but to let. Original features consist of a window in the S. wall and a vestige of window in the W. gable. In Englefield's time there were signs of other features, and the S. wall was 111 ft. long ; now, however, only a small portion

[1] It is in so bad a case that the Victoria County History and *Archaeological Journal* (1924) descriptions cannot even agree concerning its cardinal points. Both are wrong and not even consistent.

of the building remains, and in a most mutilated condition. The S. window is still good enough internally to deserve careful preservation, but if this is not done immediately, it will be too late. The window is boarded outside, but shows a segmental rear-arch supported by internal jamb-shafts, foliated capitals,[1] and roll-moulded imposts. The hall was on the first floor, and there was originally a hood-string at that level across the frontage in association with the windows.

The house was built c. 1180, judging from architectural evidence. Its misleading name dates to Englefield whose 'fond conjecture' it was that from this hall Canute with his courtiers viewed the rising tide, and from it descended to the beach 'to repress by a striking and impressive lesson, their impious flattery.'

References : *Archaeologia* xiv (1808), p. 84. H. C. Englefield (read 1801): 'Account of an Ancient Building in Southampton." Elevation, measured drawings of windows, etc.
H. C. Englefield, *A Walk through Southampton* (1801 ed.), pp. 49–54; (1805 ed.), pp. 50–54, also 97–104 (Reprint of S.A. paper and one elevation).
J. S. Davies, *A History of Southampton* (1883), pp.94–5, note.
Turner and Parker, pp. 32–35.
Arch. Journal IV (1847), p. 10. (As Turner and Parker, with illustration of window.)

N.B.—The last two references call it 'The King's House,' which makes it liable to confusion with 'King John's House.' The quay near it was not constructed till the thirteenth century, thus it was not 'our quay in front of our houses' which was ordered to be repaired in the Close Roll of 1222.[2]

HAMPSHIRE: SOUTHAMPTON—KING JOHN'S HOUSE. (Plates ii, viii A, Fig. 3.)

King John's House (or Palace) is a partial ruin in the grounds of the Tudor House Museum, and lies next to Blue Anchor Postern on the West Wall behind the three southernmost bays of the Arcade. It was built c. 1150.

Norman features are found in the N. and W. walls which are alone original; these are of coursed rubble in Isle of Wight limestone. The W. wall is common to both town and house enclosures, is thicker than the N. wall of the house, and was probably built first. Both walls thin some 9 in. at first-floor level to form a ledge for the joists of the hall floor. Three windows of this hall remain, and are simple two-lights with a mid-shaft only; the abacus of the latter is balanced by jamb-imposts, and the capitals have incised scalloping or an early palm-leaf type. Internally the jambs are straight and the

[1] These bear a strong resemblance to the capitals at Merton Hall.

[2] F. J. C. Hearnshaw and Macdonald Lucas, *Description and History of Tudor House and of the Norman House traditionally known as 'King John's Palace'—Southampton* (1932), p. 12.

rear-arch round-headed, plain in the N. and with an edge-roll in the W. windows ; there are rebates for shutters, and the mullions retain holes through which pegs were inserted to keep the shutters in place.[1] In the N. wall a fireplace is set in a slight projection ; it

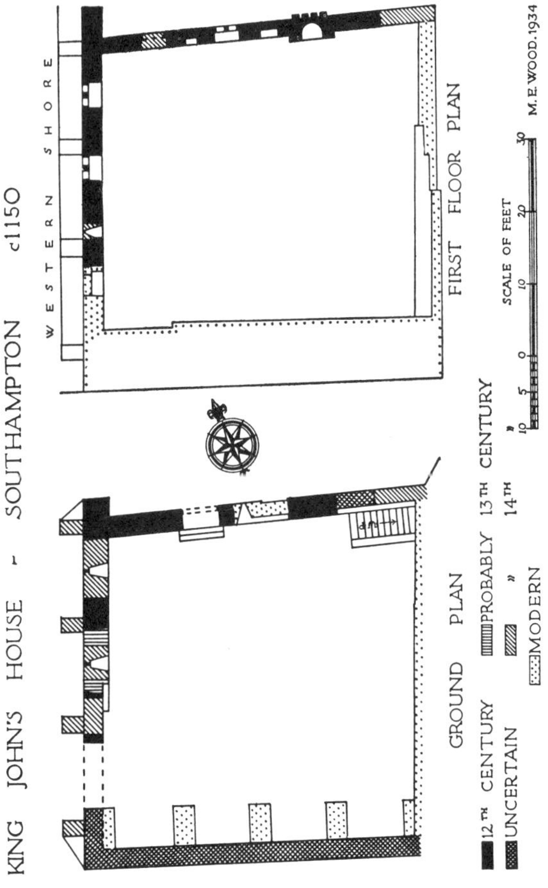

FIG. 3

has jamb-shafts, with scallop capitals, and the springing voussoirs, still in position, indicate that the arch was segmental. There was probably a cylindrical chimney, for although the flue is mutilated it is curved and tapers in the same way as at Christchurch ; however,

[1] A thirteenth-century bell capital is placed on the sill of the N. window and on first sight appears as part of the mullion.

here the supporting buttress does not extend to the ground outside, but is corbelled out some 8 ft. up the wall. On either side of the N. window is an aumbrey or lamp-stand, the E. one being rebated for a door. In the basement a N. doorway opens onto Blue Anchor Lane; the outer arch is original with a round head and chamfered hood-mould. The floor and roof have gone.

In 1337 the French sacked Southampton and King John's House was probably ruined then, and has changed little ever since. At any rate it seems to have been disused as a residence after that date. As a precaution against a repetition of the raid, the town wall was strengthened with machicolations in the form of an arcade,[1] and the openings blocked on that side. In the basement two fourteenth-century loops were inserted, the southernmost not in the blocking of the original round-arched opening, but in the segmental arch of a second period, possibly the thirteenth century. The W. wall, however, has been greatly disturbed and is most puzzling (see plan), the N. wall is less intricate but also disturbed in parts. The drawing of c. 1851, in Turner and Parker, shows a blocked doorway where the blunt lancet loop is now. Possibly the rear arch of the latter was cut down at some modern period to serve as an extra doorway when the basement was divided; otherwise there seems no reason for its position a yard from the entrance door. At first-floor level there are disturbances in the masonry suggesting a blocked window at its W. end. The S. arches are modern and the E. wall rebuilt recently. Thus the wall passage mentioned by Turner and Parker no longer exists, though the small loop that lit it still remains.

The sole survival of two adjoining walls, and no signs of a stone partition make it difficult to determine whether these walls contained a hall and solar, or a hall alone. The size of the house as suggested by its N. and W. walls, and the dissimilarity of the windows on each, seem, however, to indicate a division, and the fireplace and plain window may have belonged to the hall, the W. windows with roll moulded rear-arches to the solar. The adjacent Tudor house is built on Norman foundations, and possibly the present King John's House formed part of a large block.

The house was built c. 1150 and obviously not by King John. It is also extremely doubtful that he ever lived here. The building was more probably the house of a merchant with business on the western quay, for the large W. arches would give an easy means of transport there of goods, possibly wine or wool, stored in the basement.[2]

With regard to the origin of the name Professor F. J. C. Hearnshaw gives a complete solution of the problem in the guide to the Tudor House Museum. He attributes the rise of the King John idea to J. Duthy's *Sketches of Hampshire* (published 1839), agrees with him that neither the castle nor Canute's Palace is meant by the writers of the thirteenth-century Close Rolls when they refer to

[1] Probably of re-used material from the destroyed Norman dwelling-houses within.

[2] Hearnshaw, *Tudor House*, p. 13.

'the quay in front of our houses,' but disagrees that King John's House is meant instead, as the West Quay opposite it was the town quay, not the King's. The King's houses were outbuildings on the castle quay which belonged to the King. Also, King John, when he visited Southampton, would stay at the castle, and not at an undefended low-lying house nearby.

Condition : In modern times the building has been put to various uses, including those of a coal-store and stable. It was bought c. 1885 by Mr. W. F. G. Spranger, under whom it was restored by Messrs. T. E. Dymond and E. Cooper Poole, and various windows unblocked. In 1911 Mr. Spranger sold it at a low price to the Borough Council, and it is now well cared for as part of the Tudor House Museum.

References : H. C. Englefield, *A Walk through Southampton* (1801 ed.), pp. 69–70, Pls. ii, vi; (1805 ed.), pp. 68–69, pls. ii, vi.[1]
J. Duthy, *Sketches of Hampshire* (1839).
Turner and Parker (1851), pp. 34–37, illustrations and plan.
Brit. Arch. Assoc. Journal XXI (1865), pp. 290–2, note by E. Kell.
Arch. Journal XXIX (1872), p. 373 (note).
J. S. Davies, *A History of Southampton* (1883), pp. 91–92 (note).
Hants Field Club ii (1890–3), p. 365, description by G. W. Minns and drawings.
V.C.H. Hants iii (1908), p. 1500 (note).
W. Dale, *Story of the Historic Buildings of Southampton* (1931 ed.), pp. 13–14 (note).
F. J. C. Hearnshaw and R. Macdonald Lucas, *Descriptions and History of Tudor House and of the Norman House traditionally known as 'King John's Palace' in the County Borough of Southampton* (9th ed. 1932), obtainable from the Tudor House Museum, pp. 4–7, 11–15.

(N.B. The date of Duthy's book is therein misprinted.)

HAMPSHIRE : SOUTHAMPTON—SMALLER HOUSE OFF BLUE ANCHOR LANE, not extant but illustrated and planned.

The building stood opposite to King John's House, but has been destroyed except for some foundations in the yard of a block of workmen's flats. The chief feature was a Norman doorway.

References : Turner and Parker, pp. 34–36, plan and illustration.

[1] Englefield shows a third two-light window in the third bay of the Arcade S. of Blue Anchor Postern. Now blocked modern openings alone remain.

HAMPSHIRE: SOUTHAMPTON-VAULT ON THE WESTERN SHORE, 'Corporation Vault' or 'Cellarium.' (Plate xii B, Fig. 4.)

This is an empty vault belonging to the Corporation,[1] and situated on the West Esplanade, S. of the Castle Watergate. Original features consist of a barrel vault with traces of ribbing supported by water-leaf corbels, of which six out of an original sixteen remain. The ribbing is said to have been later than the vault, and thus contemporary with the corbels, late twelfth century. The loop has been enlarged and the doorway is modern. The ribs were destroyed c. 1775. In spite of enriched corbels this was probably a royal warehouse only.

SOUTHAMPTON-VAULT ON THE WESTERN SHORE

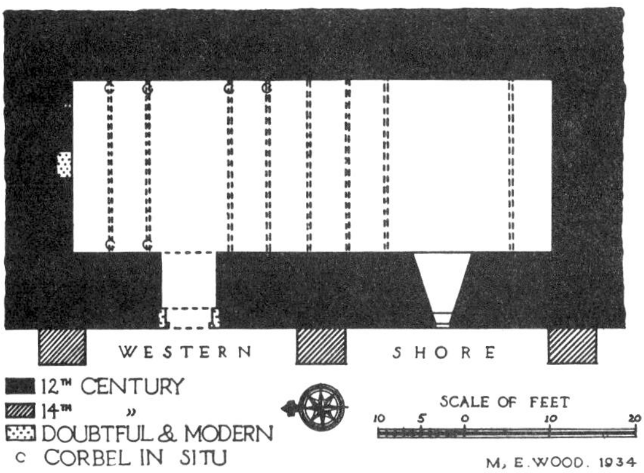

FIG. 4

References: Notes in the following—
H. C. Englefield, *A Walk through Southampton* (1805), p. 72.
Brit. Arch. Assoc. Journal xxi (1865), p. 286 (E. Kell).
Arch. Journal XXIX (1872), p. 376.
J. S. Davies, *A History of Southampton* (1883), p. 74.
Hants Field Club iv (1898–1903), p. 82 (G. W. Minns).
V.C.H. Hants iii (1908), pp. 497–8.
W. Dale, *Story of Some of the Historical Buildings of Southampton* (1931 ed.), p. 21.
Hearnshaw and Lucas, *Tudor House and King John's Palace* (1932 ed.), p. 12.

Remarks: There are other traces of twelfth-century buildings on the W. wall of Southampton. Like King John's House they would have been built against the town wall but

[1] The key is obtainable from the Tudor House Museum.

now the only features that remain are blocked round arches in the N. bays of the fourteenth-century arcade.

HAMPSHIRE: SOUTHAMPTON—HOUSE IN ST. MICHAEL'S SQUARE PASSAGE.

S. of St. Michael's Church, in a narrow passage running from St. Michael's Square to French Street there is a house now a greengrocer's shop. A drawing published by the Hampshire Field Club shows that it originally had an interesting front elevation, containing three semicircular arches, the central of which led to a barrel vaulted cellar. Nothing recognisable remains—for the stone front was removed in 1897, and the place largely rebuilt in 1906.

References : *Hants Field Club* vi, supplement (1913), p. 1.
Description by G. W. Minns with plan and illustrations.
V.C.H. Hants iii (1908), p. 491 (note).
Englefield : *A Walk through Southampton* (1805 ed.), pp. 56–61 (note).

HAMPSHIRE: CHRISTCHURCH CASTLE HALL, THE NORMAN HOUSE. (Plates iii A, ix C, Fig. 5.)

The castle hall now stands in the garden of the King's Head Hotel, and its E. wall is washed by the river Avon. Architectural evidence suggests a date c. 1160, thus it was probably built by Richard de Redvers, second Earl of Devon, who held the castle 1155–1162, or by his son Baldwin (d. 1180). The walls are of random rubble, Purbeck stone being the chief constituent, while Binstead and Freshwater stone are used for the ashlar dressings; the E. wall is the thickest as it was also the curtain, and there is a shallow plinth on the W. wall; the S. gable survives to its full height. The hall was on the first floor, but many of its features are mutilated, especially the fireplace. The chimney, however, is intact; it is cylindrical and supported by a flat buttress stepped up to its junction with the shaft. The windows are of the usual two-light form, rebated for shutters, and originally had jamb-shafts. Three are still good externally, the N. window and two on the E. wall,[1] and show round-headed lights and an enclosing arch with out-turned chevron ornament. The N. window is especially prominent, being at the upper end of the hall; instead of a plain chamfered hood the inner order is here also elaborated with chevron and has diaper-pattern on the hood; there is a grotesque head over the outer arch, and the rear-arch has an angle roll and groove treatment, now concealed by ivy. The entrance doorway is narrow and round-headed; the external stair to it has disappeared. In the basement three loops remain, and another has been cut through to form a doorway. There is no evidence of a sub-vault, but joist-holes for the hall floor are visible on the E. and W. walls; beneath are put-

[1] Grose shows a third E. window over the river-gate, also a small attic window separated by a string-course from the NE. two-light opening.

log holes. On the W. end of the S. wall (first-floor level) a segmental-headed doorway led to an annexe, now destroyed. This opening is probably original, but not that on the other end of the wall, which turned E. into a garderobe. There are traces of a newel stair at the NE. corner, which may have been contained in a square turret of slight projection.

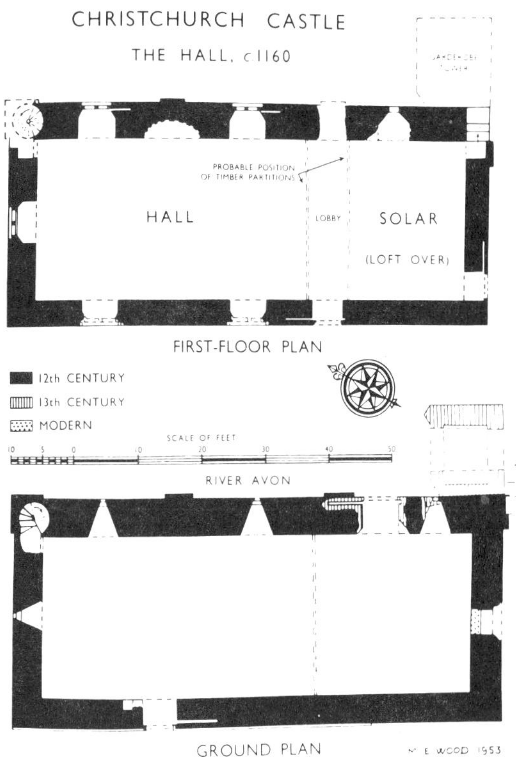

FIG. 5

The garderobe tower is a later medieval addition. It is in ruins and overgrown, but the round arches of its channel are still good. The river-gate has an outer segmental arch, and is probably contemporary with the garderobe. In this corner (SE.) there seems to have been three periods of building, all medieval. This is the probable order :—

(1) First there was no exit to the water, and the loops formed the only openings in the E. wall.

(2) Then the end loop was broken through to form a river-gate on its N. jamb.
(3) That doorway would be inconvenient when the garderobe tower was built and it was blocked, while the present river-gate was built well away from the tower.

Condition : Much overgrown with ivy and badly in need of preservation. There is a crack in the elaborate N. window, but the mullion has been restored.

References : *V.C.H. Hants* v (1912), p. 88, with illustrations and plan ($\frac{1}{24}$ in. scale).
(N.B. The plan is incorrect with regard to the position of the entrance doorway, and the shape of the garderobe.)
M. and C. H. B. Quennell, *Everyday Life in Anglo-Saxon, Viking and Norman Times* (1926), pp. 106–7. External and internal reconstructions, pp. 97 and 98, and a plan (with the entrance wrong).
Turner and Parker, p. 38, illustration.
N. Lloyd, illustrations, pp. 173, 328, 346.
Sir B. Fletcher, *A History of Architecture* (Batsford, 1928), illustration, p. 396.
A. Hamilton Thompson, *Military Architecture*, p. 192.
Clapham and Godfrey, *Some Famous Buildings and their Story*, pp. 70, 73–75.
F. Grose, *Antiquities of England and Wales*, suppl., vol. v (1777), p. 79 (1776, engraving).

HEREFORDSHIRE : HEREFORD — THE GREAT HALL OF THE BISHOPS (Plate xi B)

this dates from c. 1160, but is much disguised. It was originally a wooden hall with nave and aisles. Above the eighteenth-century ceiling can be seen a timber arch of the E. nave arcade and two scalloped capitals of the destroyed nave arches. Part of a pier can also be seen in a room on the W. side.

References : *R.C.H.M. Herefordshire* i (1931), pp. 116–7, Pl. 24.
Included in a coloured plan of the Cathedral ($\frac{1}{24}$ in. scale).
J. Clayton, drawing of hall.
(Author of *Ancient Timber Edifices in England.*)

HUNTINGDONSHIRE : HEMINGFORD GREY MANOR HOUSE. (Plate ix A and B, Fig. 6.)

The main block dates from c. 1150 and was a first-floor hall. Original features consist of the remains of a fireplace (now in a cupboard) ; an entrance doorway in the end wall (an unusual position) and partly filled by a modern window ; and four Norman windows, of which two are visible externally, and one has only recently been discovered.[1] The latter is a two-light window with solid tympanum and restored mullion.

[1] This NW. window does not appear in the *R.C.H.M.* plan of 1926.

References : *R.C.H.M. Hunts* (1926), pp. 135–6, with first-floor plan ($\frac{1}{16}$ in. scale), plates 78 and 116.
V.C.H. Hunts ii (1926), pp. 309–311, with illustration.

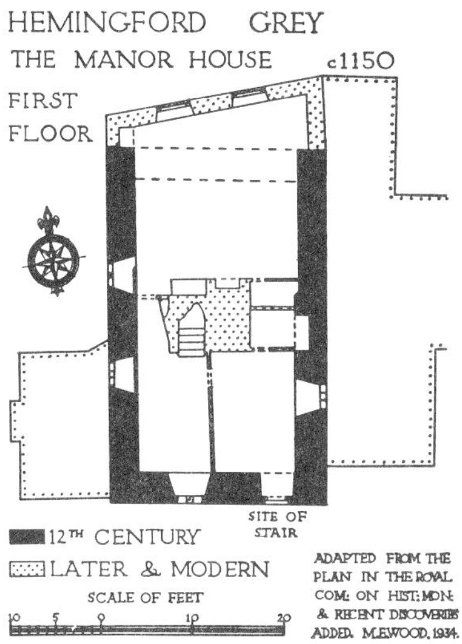

FIG. 6

KENT : MINSTER COURT (OR ABBEY).

This house has a curious plan, apparently semi-monastic, but was at one time used as a grange of the Abbey of St. Augustine, Canterbury. It compromises a W. block with herring-bone walling, a later hall to the N. and a church (excavated) to the S. The hall is probably contemporary with the church and dates from c. 1120; it has one-light windows, buttresses, and an external string-course. A twelfth-century passage runs between the W. wing and the church tower, and is now called the ' Saxon Cloister,' and used as a chapel.

Reference : *Arch. Journal* LXXXVI (1929), pp. 213–223.
P. K. Kipps, for description of the hall, W. wing and excavation of the church carried out by Mr. A. W. Clapham, F.S.A. and the author. Illustrations and plan ($\frac{1}{24}$ in. scale).

KENT : WEST MALLING—' PREBENDAL HOUSE.'

Original features include two chevron windows at first-floor level, dating c. 1140–50.

Reference : Article not yet published by F. C. Elliston Erwood, F.S.A., with plan and photographs.

KENT: LUDDESDOWN COURT.

Luddesdown is a village just S. of Cobham. The house is next to the church. It is, however, a doubtful example, though claimed to be of Norman even Saxon fabric. The hall fireplace is thirteenth century and later, and the quoins remaining on the NE. even suggest the fourteenth century, the date of several interesting drawings on the plaster of the hall. Many of the arches have segmental heads; these occur in the twelfth century but are not usual. The corbel, however, of the round arch under the solar fireplace resembles one in the cellar of Aaron's House. A 'columbarium' is attached to the building. The roof fell in 1913, and the house has now one of corrugated iron.

References: W. B. Peake, *Luddesdown, the Story of a Kentish Manor* (1928). (Sketches from this are printed with notes in a booklet 'Luddesdown Court, A Norman Manor House,' obtainable, price 6d., from the office of the *South Eastern Gazette*, Maidstone. Ground and first-floor plans by Peake and W. Mitchell.)
N. Lloyd, illustration of fireplace, p. 434.

KENT: EYNSFORD CASTLE HALL

The so-called keep seems to have been the hall. It is much overgrown, but still contains loops and traces of a spiral stair. The basement was divided by a cross wall, and the fireplace may be original.

References: *Archaeologia* XXVII (1835), pp. 391–7 (E. Crecy, plans).
H. Sands, *Some Kentish Castles* (1907), p. 36.

KENT: CHILHAM CASTLE—REMAINS OF LATE ELEVENTH-CENTURY BUILDING.

Remains of an early hall are incorporated in the base of the castle fore-building. It was excavated in 1926 by Mr. A. W. Clapham, F.S.A.

Reference: *Antiq. Journal* VIII (1928), pp. 350–3. Plan ($\frac{1}{24}$ in.) and illustrations. (The plan is also printed in *Arch. Journal* LXXXVI, 303.)

LEICESTERSHIRE: LEICESTER CASTLE HALL.

The hall was built c. 1150 of Dane Hill sandstone, and originally divided by timber posts into nave and aisles. It is now used as Assize Courts, for which it was greatly altered in the nineteenth century. In both court rooms some of the existing roof is ancient, and may be original in the case of the tie-beams and struts. The ties have chamfered under-edges, and apparently rested on square timber piers to which they were also bound by struts. Other struts stand on the tie-beams themselves to support the principal rafters. The W. aisle has been walled off, and the roofing renewed, but the

E. line of piers is still apparent through the presence of the struts and the top of the timber piers, which are lopped below and now rest on a modern beam. No capitals remain in position, so it is impossible to say how far up they occurred on the piers. Mr. Fosbrooke's reconstruction places them some two-thirds up from the ground, and certainly the detached scalloped capital now exhibited has no abacus, but the post continuing above it. There are two tall chevron windows, much restored, on the S. wall, also a re-set pointed arch in chevron on the W.

Condition : Much disguised.

References : Unpublished plan, by W. Keay, F.R.I.B.A.
Reconstruction, by T. H. Fosbrooke.
J. Thompson, *An Account of Leicester Castle* (1859), illustration.
G. T. Clark, *Medieval Military Architecture* (1884), ii, 182.
T. Fielding Johnson, *Glimpses of Ancient Leicester* (1896), pp. 48, 134–7 (note).
C. J. Billson, *Medieval Leicester* (1920), pp. 41, 200–1 (note).
Archaeological Journal xc (1933), p. 368 (photograph of capital, p. 365) (note).

LINCOLNSHIRE : LINCOLN—ST. MARY'S GUILD OR JOHN O'GAUNT'S STABLES. (Plates iv A, xii A, xiii B, Fig. 7.)

It is now a builder's yard (385, High Street). The present enclosure is oblong, bounded by the entrance range to W. and a twentieth-century brick house to E. S. is a recent stone range with workshops, and N. are two curious buildings in re-used material but of different dates. That nearest the entrance was built some forty years ago and is of little interest except for re-used chevron in the jambs of the S. doorway and a window. The adjoining block is earlier, and has been considered an original 'Norman house.' Its N. wall is twelfth century, especially on the ground floor, and has two windows, both partially blocked, round-headed, and deeply splayed ; the ground-floor window is now used as a cupboard, the first-floor one is almost hidden by lumber but seems to have traces of sculpture near it. However, the parallel wall on to the yard is much thinner, and built up with Norman stones, two shafted windows and a buttress.[1] The buttress is the height of two storeys, and against it between the windows is a flat-topped fireplace, not easily visible, which if only it could be freed of lumber, might be used to date this curious sham-Norman house. The house must be old enough to create a Norman tradition for even Turner and Parker were deceived by it.[2] The Norman N. wall is completed with probably seventeenth-century brick on the first floor, and this may give a clue to the

[1] There is also a small niche with some mutilated carving, and a splayed opening behind.

[2] Also Sir Banister Fletcher—Mr. W. Watkins was apparently the first to discover the fraud.

construction of the rest of the house, for the E. gable is built of the same material.[1] If it was due to the antiquarian instinct, to fake a Norman house is a curious feature of the seventeenth and eighteenth

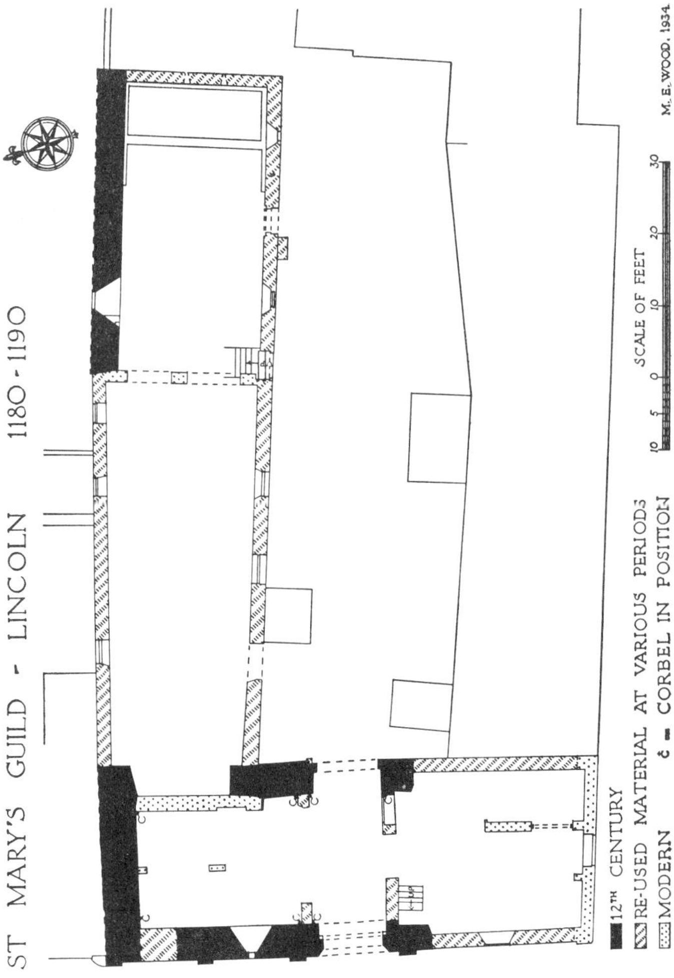

FIG. 7

centuries and caused by the nearness of Jew's House ; but on the other hand the resemblance may be accidental, and the arrangement

[1] The roof is old with tie and scissor-beams ; it rests on the brick wall, thus is either contemporaneous with it or later.

based on convenience. That is the more likely view. There is some re-used medieval work in the modern S. range.

But most original features remain in the N. half of the entrance range (1180-90), and include an elaborate gateway and string-course. The doorway has mutilated heads of bishops on the stop-chamfer of the jambs; there is a slightly pointed arch but the outer rings to it are round-headed; these include a hood with rosette ornament, and beneath a line of dog-tooth in hollow-chamfer, two rings of roll-moulding cut with a hollow on the under-side somewhat akin to the quirked ogee. Above are two projecting heads resting on an ornate string-course carved with scrolls, acanthus, and fantastic creatures. The wall is 4 ft. 7 in. in thickness, built in large blocks of ashlar oolite, nicely squared and coursed; the flat buttresses flanking the gate and N. of it are original. Inside are remnants of arcading on the N. wall at first-floor level; the halves of two wide semicircular arches remain, supported by an extremely lovely capital of wing or acanthus design. It was hidden behind a modern wall till just recently, hence the excellent state of preservation. Near it is a smaller capital, also beautifully carved, and a doorway. There are traces of an internal string on the W. wall and the bases of window shafts, but the upper storey has mostly gone. It was apparently a first-floor hall over a basement.[1] The latter was possibly vaulted as in Mr. W. Watkins' reconstruction; some corbels remaining give him a clue to a ribbed vault, probably quadripartite and of five oblong bays, the central one forming the entrance. Other evidence, however, suggests that the corbels merely supported wall posts, and the compartments are too long to be easily vaulted. But in the fragmentary condition of the building, the whole matter is one of doubt. The ground-floor was certainly lit by loop windows; a perfect example remains in the W. wall, splayed to a round-headed rear arch. N. of it another opening, probably a doorway, has been blocked.

The entrance range has been curtailed; a pen-and-ink sketch dated 1784 shows the Norman work, the later rebuild (with square headed windows) and adjoining but in the same line a building with a two-light window, almost pointed, on the S. wall. This portion abutted on the churchyard, and was taken down when the present Sibthorpe Street was made. A print of 1831 (J. Salmon) also indicates a longer W. range.

Mr. Watkins sees in St. Mary's Guild a training school for masons, and it is just possible. The whole history of the place is obscure, but it denotes from its scale and decoration an owner or owners of importance. John of Gaunt's fourteenth-century palace used to stand opposite, and there seems no reason to doubt that the Norman building, then old and decayed, might have been used as its stables. That would explain the alternative name to St. Mary's Guild.

[1] The wooden staircase is on the site of a newel stair, for the wall curves to meet it above.

References : *Journal of Royal Institute of British Architects*, third series, xx (1913), W. Watkins, F.R.I.B.A. The buildings of St. Mary's Guild, Lincoln, illustration, ground and first-floor plans, reconstructed plans and elevations.[1]
St. Mary's Guild, Lincoln and Medieval Builders, third series, xxi, no. 9 (1914).
Turner and Parker (1851), p. 40, illustration.
Sir B. Fletcher, *A History of Architecture*, p. 396, illustration.
Arch. Journal LXVI (1909), p. 352.

LINCOLNSHIRE : LINCOLN—JEW'S HOUSE. (Plates V A, xiii A, Fig. 8.)

Jew's House (15, The Strait) is probably the best known of the Norman houses. It was a first-floor hall, built 1170–80. The walls are of ashlar, in large blocks of yellow oolite, but the roof and attics are modern. It is now a furniture-shop, and has been much altered and sub-divided. Additions include modern shop-fronts, cellar, and wings to the north.

The house was traditionally owned in the twelfth century by one of the rich Jews of Lincoln. In 1290 the Jewess Belaset of Wallingford was condemned for clipping the King's coin, and is said to have lived here.

The street front shows most original features. These include an elaborate ground-floor entrance, and two windows to the hall above. The hall fireplace is blocked, but the chimney buttress still exists, supported on the hood-mould of the entrance arch. This doorway is of two orders, the jamb-shafts have gone, but their foliated capitals remain ; these have double-grooved and chamfered abaci on which rests a semicircular arch richly carved with interlaced or basket pattern ; the tympanum is modern and the jambs partially repaired, however there still remains some dog-tooth ornament which originally flanked the jamb-shafts. The hall windows are mutilated two-lights, originally five-shafted, but the mid-shafts have gone completely and modern sashes inserted. The S. window is the better preserved, with inner order and jamb-shafts still partially *in situ* ; the abacus of the outer order is continued inwards and supports two round-headed lights, edged with roll-moulding ; the outer arch is more elaborately enriched with rolls and hollow mouldings with pellets ; the hood mould is continued as a string-course across the frontage, and is carved with cable-pattern on the face and palmette on the chamfer. A second string runs at the level of the sills : it has various bead and roll mouldings, the upper of which has a cable turned with pellets.

Inside there is little to see beyond three plain doorways on the original N. wall, two on the ground, one on the first floor. The

[1] The reconstructed plan is based on a symmetry not usual in medieval buildings, but the entrance gateway pre-supposes the existence of some sort of courtyard.

modern brick-lined entrance passage may denote the site of earlier wooden partitions, as it leads to another and loftier doorway in the back wall of the original building. The last-mentioned opening is rebated internally indicating the former existence of some kind of annexe, either in timber or stone. A thick wall almost at right angles to the opening may be Norman, or if not, certainly medieval, perhaps on the line of twelfth-century timber work. The angle between this and the long N. wall of the house is covered by a low curved remnant of masonry, and there is another old wall to the E. of this outwork and a second, possibly medieval, to the W. The result is three parallel walls, joining the Norman hall near its centre,

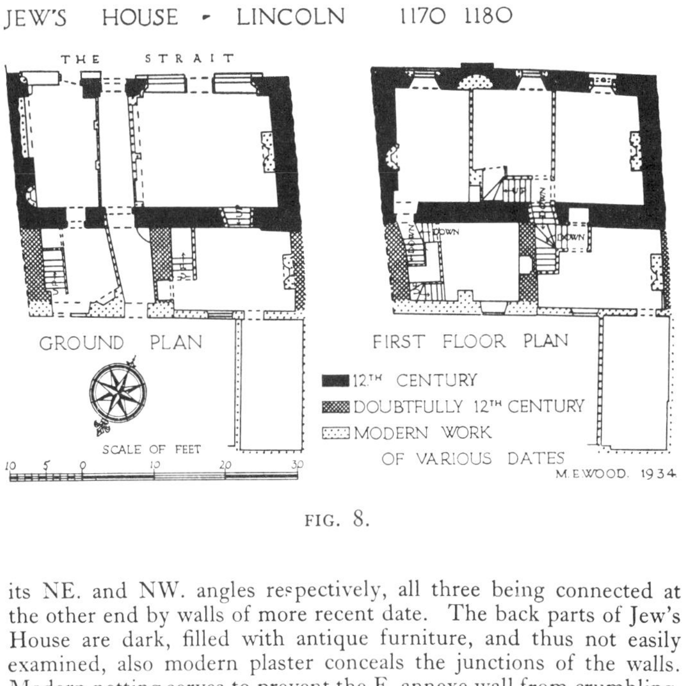

FIG. 8.

its NE. and NW. angles respectively, all three being connected at the other end by walls of more recent date. The back parts of Jew's House are dark, filled with antique furniture, and thus not easily examined, also modern plaster conceals the junctions of the walls. Modern netting serves to prevent the E. annexe wall from crumbling, and makes investigation there almost impossible. At first-floor level, this wall has either fallen inwards or is built against the E. chamfer of the hall doorway in a manner suggesting its being of a later build.

Thus the plan at Jew's House is obscure, but the following suggestion may tentatively be put forward concerning the arrangement. The family entered from the street by the elaborate ground-floor doorway, proceeded along a narrow central passage between store-rooms, and after leaving the main block, by the N. door, entered an annexe possibly a kitchen, from which wooden stairs led up to the NE. door of the hall above. This staircase probably mounted at right angles to the wall of the hall on the lines of the present steps from lower to upper workrooms, otherwise it might have interfered with the door to the E. part of the basement. The last-named apartment has a curious feature in its E. wall, a wide low arch 8¼ feet broad by 5½ feet high, partially blocked. This blocking probably took place when Jew's Court was built next door. There is a double (not a single) wall between the two houses; thus the low arch did not lead into Jew's Court as it has been suggested. The street doorway to the E. basement is later medieval, and possibly replaced the E. arch. This would make Jew's Court considerably later than Jew's House. The walls are c. 2 ft. 8 in. in thickness.

Condition : Many of its features are mutilated, but what remains is worth cleaning and preservation.

References : Slight notes occur in—
Turner and Parker (1851), p. 41, with illustration.
E. M. Sympson, *Lincoln* (1907), p. 88, and illustration p. 80.
N. Lloyd, p. 172, and photographs pp. 305, 328.
Sir B. Fletcher, *A History of Architecture* (illustration p. 412).

LINCOLNSHIRE: LINCOLN—JEW'S COURT. (Fig. 9.)

Jew's Court adjoins the Jew's House to the E. It is doubtfully twelfth-century, and certainly later than Jew's House, the E. door of which was blocked when Jew's Court was built (see above). The cellar and E. and W. walls of the upper floors seem the earliest portions. Additions include a solar, said to be later medieval, three Tudor windows, and twentieth-century partitions. The house is held by some to have been a synagogue, by others the place of martyrdom of little St. Hugh of Lincoln in 1255. But the well 'in which the body was concealed' has now been removed as an eighteenth-century 'forgery.'

Condition : Very much modernised.

References : T. S. Howitt, *Jew's Court and the legend of little St. Hugh of Lincoln* (1911), illustration and plans of basement and first floor. (Plan before recent alterations.)
Sympson: *Lincoln* (1907), p. 88 (note).

LINCOLNSHIRE: LINCOLN—HOUSE NEAR ST. BENEDICT'S CHURCH, not extant.

This house mentioned in Turner and Parker (p. 41) had three late Norman doorways in the position of those at Appleton. It has lately been removed, and a Marks and Spencer's stores occupies the site.

LINCOLNSHIRE: LINCOLN—AARON THE JEW'S HOUSE. (Plate V B.)

Aaron the Jew's House consists of a double block of buildings comprising 46 and 47 Steep Hill, and 1 Christ's Hospital Terrace. The architectural evidence suggests a date 1170–80, which fits in

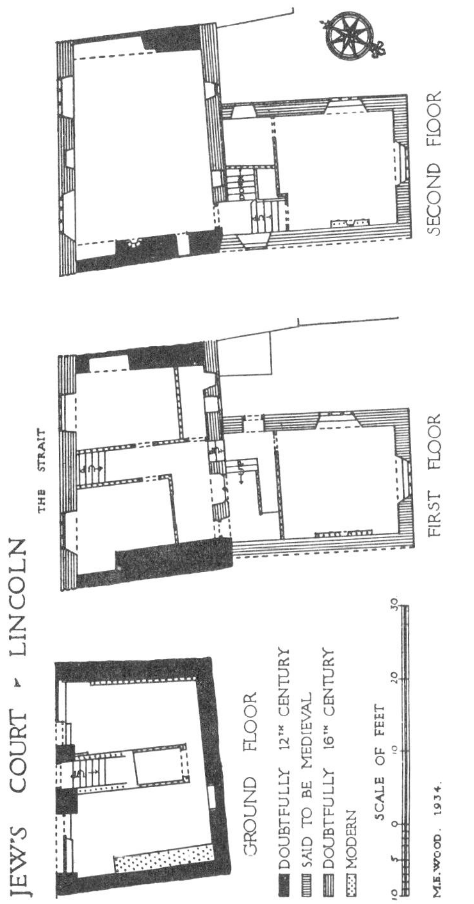

FIG. 9.

with the traditional ownership by Aaron the Jew, who lived in Lincoln c. 1166–1186. The S. wall is partially faced with brick, but retains a fragment of string-course; the W. wall contains an entrance arch with terminal grotesques to the hood and originally a fireplace buttress above, also a re-set and restored Norman window said to have been found in pieces in a ground-floor recess in 1878. There is a good barrel vault and an aumbrey in the semi-underground cellar. The steps to the latter are doubtfully original, and a lintel with the date 1107 in modern characters has been inserted into the doorway at the foot; but an original square-headed recess, occurs above the steps.

It seems to have been a large building, contained in walls between 3 ft. and 4 ft. in thickness. The internal arrangement is, however, so altered and mutilated that the original plan is obscure.

Condition : Very much disguised. A thorough exploration would be interesting, with the removal of modern wall-paper. The walls slope very much, and are often out of the parallel.

References : Sympson, *Lincoln* (1907), pp. 89–90, illustration p. 368 (note).
Turner and Parker, p. 42 (note).

LINCOLNSHIRE : BOOTHBY PAGNELL—MANOR HOUSE. (Plates iii B, vi, vii A, viii B, x C, Fig. 10.)

The Norman house is an unoccupied building in the grounds of the modern manor-house. It was built c. 1200, and was originally two-storeyed, consisting of a hall and solar over vaulted basements, but a modern attic floor has been inserted, a wing and out-house added to the W, and the gables and roof are also modern. The walls are of coursed rubble oolite with ashlar dressings.

The house is especially interesting as it contains a solar, and in one building block with the hall.

The E. elevation contains the original entrances to the cellars, both with a shouldered arch; but the doorway to the solar basement is now partially blocked with a modern window inserted. None of the cellar windows are original, but like all ground-floor openings, have relieving-arches above. An external staircase, modern but probably on the site of the old, leads to the hall entrance, a round-headed doorway with chamfered jambs, and hood terminating in a shell or curl ornament. There is a good Norman window to the solar, with two round-headed lights divided by a polygonal mid-shaft and capital, and crowned by a solid tympanum bound by a chamfered semicircular hood-mould. A similar E. window to the hall has been replaced by a fifteenth-century four-light window, and was apparently moved to the S. wall to light a small entrance apartment when the hall was partitioned.

The S. wall contains this re-set window breaking the string-course, and a similar two-light in its original position, not quite central to the frontage. The S. basement entrance is modern.

The W. side shows no ancient features except a blocked window to the hall, and a cylindrical chimney supported on a gabled plinth and stepped buttress. The stone-work of the plinth indicates that the original roof was steeper. There is little of interest on the N. wall.

Internally the ground-floor consists of two vaulted cellars. That under the solar has a barrel vault placed at right angles to the ribbed vault of the adjoining room beneath the hall. The latter is larger, and divided into two virtually square compartments by semicircular transverse and diagonal arches supported on six cushion corbels chamfered to match the ribs. Here the joggled lintel of the entrance has been questioned, but it seems original and resembles the lintel-treatment of the hall fireplace.

The first floor contains the hall and solar divided by a stone wall pierced by a doorway having a round-headed arch supported on corbels. The half-timber partitioning is old but of doubtful date: it now divides the original hall into a large room opening N. into

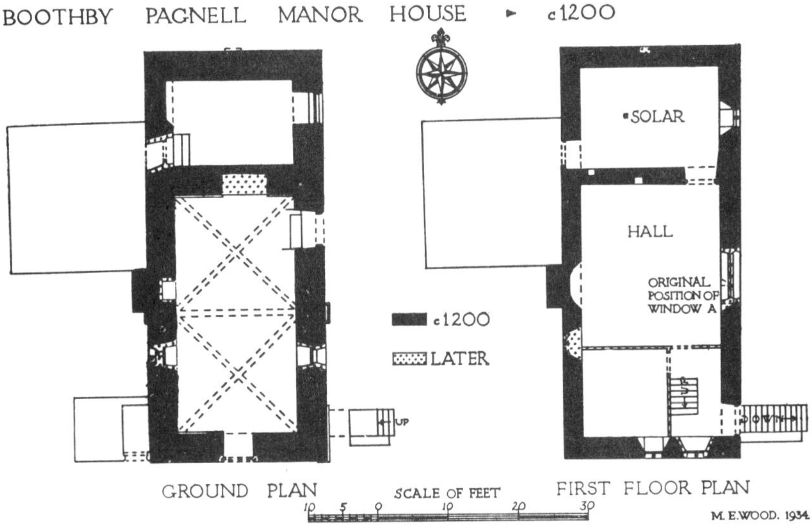

FIG. 10.

the solar and at the S. end two smaller rooms, the W. one lit by the original S. window, the E. one containing the Norman entrance, a modern staircase to the attic and the inserted twelfth-century window mentioned above. The present hall has a perpendicular window to the E. and beneath it the foot-rest of the original Norman window, an aumbrey with rebated triangular head on the N. wall, and on the W. the twelfth-century stone fireplace. The latter has a projecting hood resting on a pear-shaped string and joggled lintel, in turn supported by tapering corbels. The hearth is confined by a slight 'fender' of stone, possibly original. The solar has a small aumbrey on the S. wall, a W. doorway of doubtful date, and on the E. an original window with segmental rear-arch and window-seats. All the windows are grooved for shutters.

The width of wall is 4 ft. on the ground floor, and c. 2 ft. 9 in. on the first.

A moat, now dry, surrounds the house.

Condition : Very good. One of the best preserved of Norman houses.

References : No very detailed account or plan exists.
Bucks Archit. and Arch. Soc. Rec. xii (1927–1933), pp. 299–301, F. W. Bull, illustrated.
Turner and Parker, p. 52, note and illustrations.
A. Hamilton Thompson, *Military Architecture*, pp. 190–2.
Arch. Journal LXVI (1909), p. 379 (description by A. Hamilton Thompson).
N. Lloyd, illustrations pp. 173, 329, 354, 434.
Fletcher, illustration p. 396.

LINCOLNSHIRE : STAMFORD—'NORMAN HOUSE.'

'Norman House,' 11 St. Mary's Hill, contains a twelfth-century arch opening onto a passage, and marked by a Corporation notice with the legend (in both senses): 'This Norman Arch is believed to be one of the postern gates in the town walls.' It has also been called 'Pack-House Arch,' but is really the doorway of a Norman house.

The arch is the only feature visible, and is dated by the chevron ornament to c. 1150. The Norman wall to N. is obscured by the shelves of a shop ; the wall bounding the passage to the S. may be original and is 36 ft. long.

Condition : Fair as regards the arch, but even here on the N. the outer order is mutilated and the inner order embedded in later wall.

Reference : E. M. Sympson, *Memorials of Old Lincolnshire* (1911), p. 167 (note).

LONDON AND MIDDLESEX : SOUTHWARK—HOSTELRY OF THE PRIORS OF LEWES, TWO CRYPTS, not extant but illustrated and planned.

Two crypts stood on the site now occupied by the yard of London Bridge Station. They are believed to have formed part of a hostelry of the Prior and Convent of St. Pancras, Lewes. Crypt I was demolished in 1830 to allow the approach to new London Bridge. The main room had a groined vault in four bays, with plain bands supported by responds with carved capitals. A smaller room to the NE. was also groined, and there were two other chambers to N. and NW. with barrel vaults. Crypt II was also vaulted in four bays, with one central column from which sprung plain bands supported on the walls by square responds ; the diagonal arches were not ribbed.

References : *V.C.H. Surrey* iv (1912), pp. 126–7, plan, p. 138; illustration (Crypts I and II).
Turner and Parker, p. 47, illustration (Crypt I).
Archaeologia xxiii (1831), p. 299 (Crypt I).[1] Buckler's drawings, good.
Archaeologia xxv (1834), p. 604; plan and good illustrations.[1] (Crypt II).

LONDON : CORBET COURT CRYPT—not extant but illustrated and planned before demolition.

A crypt situated in Corbet Court, near Gracechurch Street was demolished in 1872. It was the ground-floor of a large Norman house, had three aisles of two bays each and plain vaulting unribbed save for transverse and longitudinal bands. There was a wall arcade and other features included a newel stair. A projecting porch seems also to have existed.

Reference : *Brit. Arch. Assoc. Journal* xxviii (1872), p. 179. E. P. Loftus Brock, with illustrations and plan ($\frac{1}{8}$ in. scale).

LONDON : WESTMINSTER HALL.

Original features dating to William II are for the most part concealed by the work of Richard II. The hall was an aisled one of twelve bays, and had a window arcade consisting of twelve round-headed windows and lower openings in between giving on to a wall-passage with a barrel vault. Some scalloped capitals remain *in situ* but hidden, and more elaborate ones said to have come from here are to be seen at the Victoria and Albert Museum.

References : *R.C.H.M. W. London* (1925), pp. 120–3, pls. 177–179. Elevations and plan giving reconstruction of Norman arrangement.

RUTLAND : OAKHAM CASTLE HALL. (Fig. 11.)

This was rather a fortified manor-house than a castle, and a stone wall was not added to the defensive bank until the thirteenth century. The building is important as an aisled hall in stone, and as the Norman house with the most elaborate decoration. It was built c. 1190, thus shows Transitional features and an abundance of dog-tooth ornament. Nineteenth-century wings were added to N. and W. for use in its present capacity as Shire Hall. The N. wall has been altered towards the E., contains externally a curious ground string-course under which the wall recedes, and internally a projection possibly supporting a wooden stair originally. The NE. buttress has been rebuilt.

Original features include two-light windows, six cylindrical piers, and rich ornament in the form of capitals, corbels, and spandril-figures. Two finials remain in position on the gables : a centaur to the W., and in the E. what has been variously entitled ' St. George

[1] These give detailed measurements.

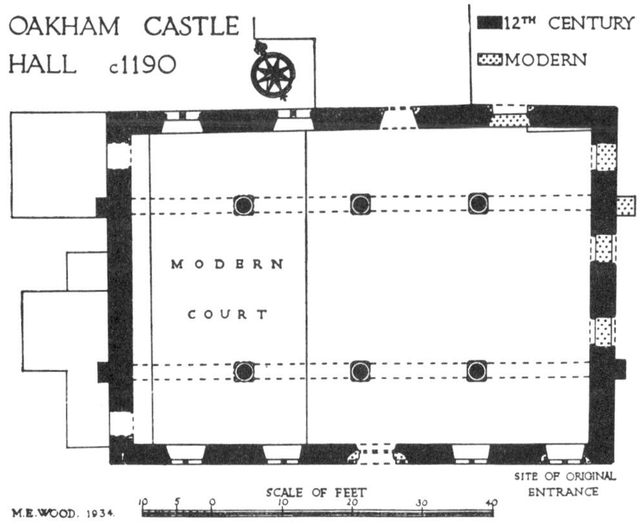

FIG. 11.

and the Dragon,'[1] 'Samson and the Lion,'[2] and 'a woman seated on the back of a scaly animal.'[3] Turner and Parker foresee the coming conflict, and prudently call it 'A figure in a long surcoat, mounted on the back of a lion or other animal.'[4]

Condition : Very good, although the entrance doorway has been moved to a central position.

References : Turner and Parker (1851), pp. 28–31, plan and many illustrations.

V. C. H. Rutland ii (1935), pp. 8–10, with plan and illustrations.

H. Avray Tipping, *English Homes* i (1921), pp. xvii–xxii, '*Country Life*' photographs.

J. A. Gotch, *The Growth of the English House* (1909), pp. 27–33, with plan and illustrations.

Thoroton Soc. Trans. xxviii (1924), p. 29 (J. Holland Walker), with illustrations.

Rutland Magazine v (1911–12), p. 80 (A. Hamilton Thompson), with illustration.

[1] J. Holland Walker in *Thoroton Soc. Trans.* xxviii, 29.

[2] *Arch. Journal*, xc (1934), p. 397 (photograph).

[3] Lloyd, p. 174.

[4] Turner and Parker, p. 31. Illustrations, p. 30.

A. Hamilton Thompson, *Military Architecture*, pp. 197–8.
Clapham and Godfrey, *Some Famous Buildings and their Story*, pp. 72–73, with plan.
N. Lloyd, illustrations pp. 174, 329, 354.
Arch. Journal xc (1934), pp. 397–398, illustrations.
Dollman, *Analysis of Ancient Domestic Architecture in Great Britain* i (1861), pl. 3 (window).

SOMERSET : SALTFORD MANOR HOUSE, OR MANOR FARM. (Plate ix D.)

Saltford is a village 5 miles NW. of Bath. The manor-house lies near the church, and is at present unoccupied. It was built c. 1150, and was apparently a first-floor hall with a later solar to the E, and a later chapel projecting to the N. The walls are of random rubble in white lias, but the S. wall is refaced (or rebuilt) and all the buttresses to N. and S. are later, also the roof and buildings projecting to the W. Roof ornaments include a stone lion over the E. (solar) gable. There are two fireplaces, bearing the dates 1645 and 1637 respectively.

Original features consist chiefly in a good chevron window on the N. wall. It is a two-light of three-shaft type : the hood is carved with double-groove and nail-head, and the covering arch with in-turned double chevron ; the round heads of the lights are bordered with a simple groove, and supported by half shafts, also with incised scallop capitals. On the same wall are the original hall and basement entrances ; both are partially blocked and have segmental arches.

The house is said to be associated with the Abbey of Keynsham in the next parish, but that was only founded in 1166, and the decoration at Saltford implies an earlier date. It was perhaps a grange, but more probably the manor-house of the Fitz Hamon or Bargouse families.

Condition : The house is in urgent need of repair, although the window is still good. The latter was discovered some fifty years ago behind a buttress by Major L. Flower, father of the present owner. The building is little known, but a survey is in progress.

References : W. J. Robinson, *West Country Manors* (Bristol, St. Stephen's Press, 1930) ; article on Saltford Manor.

SUFFOLK : BURY ST. EDMUND'S—MOYSE'S HALL. (Plates vii B, x A, Fig. 12.)

Moyse's Hall (5, St. Mary's Square) was built c. 1180, apparently as a large dwelling-house of the hall-and-solar type. In modern times it has undergone many changes, including the state of work-house and police-station, and in 1899 became the Borough Museum. It is built of flint with ashlar dressings, the S. buttresses are original but not the gables. Only the S. and W. walls are entirely Norman, being c. 3 ft. 8 in. thick on the ground, c. 3 ft. 5 in. on the first floor ; the rest are Tudor or nineteenth century, and the E. wall was rebuilt and set back when the road there was widened. A drastic restoration took place in 1858 at the hands of Sir Gilbert Scott, and the pseudo-Norman windows on the ground-floor were then inserted. There are some late medieval and Tudor features, including three fireplaces,

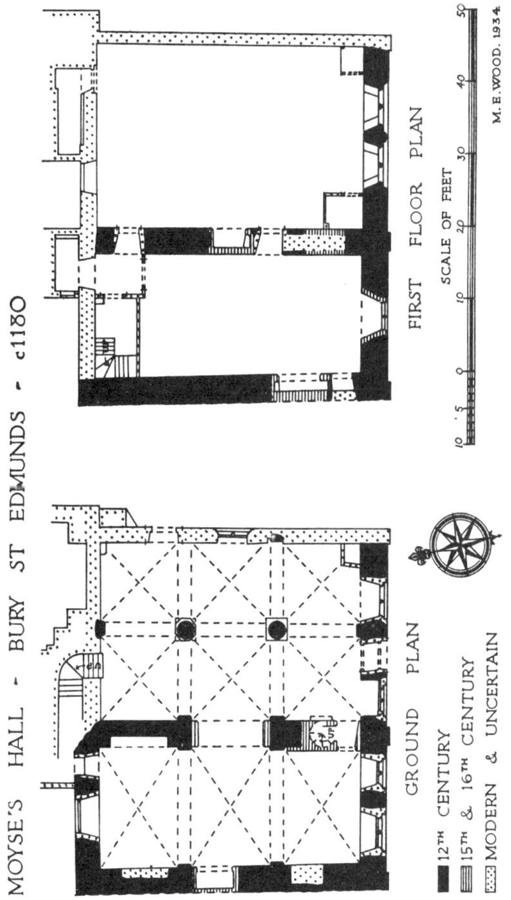

FIG. 12.

the solar window, also a brick arch and a newel stair in the twelfth-century partition wall.

Original features include a divided basement, the W. part being the smaller and formerly 8 ft. deeper than it is to-day. The latter has a roughly semicircular groined vault, in three oblong bays; there are responds to E. and W. supporting wide transverse bands alike with chamfered edges. The E. and larger part is divided into two aisles by two cylindrical piers with square rebated abaci ; from these spring wide transverse and longitudinal ribs supported by responds, two on the W. and (originally) E., and one on the N. and S. respectively. These bands have chamfered edges as have the responds, which are similar to those in the W. room. Unlike the latter the ribs here are slightly pointed, but the diagonal groins are rounded. The room is thus divided into six square bays.

Above are the hall and solar. The hall (to E.) has a pair of good late Norman windows in the S. wall. These are interesting as an example of twelfth-century rectangular lights ; each light has a covering round arch with roll and hollow mouldings, a solid tympanum, and jamb-shafts with volute capitals almost identical with those found in the Jew's House doorway and at Oakham. The rear-arches are semicircular and have a pear-shaped edge-roll. There are window-seats parallel to the splayed jambs, and external and internal string-courses, the latter continuing into a modern cupboard.

Moyse's Hall is said to have been a Jewish house or synagogue, but it more probably was connected with the Abbey, being perhaps one of the stone houses in the town that Abbot Samson bought c. 1198 to house his scholars ;[2] or even one of the stone houses that the Abbot built himself, and which the Londoners threatened to destroy.[3] If so the connection had broken by 1328, and the house was possibly an inn, judging from the earliest mention of Moyse's Hall in a lurid story quoted by Mr. Jennings.

Condition : Good in respect of the vaulting and hall windows, otherwise too much restored.

References : Turner and Parker (1851), p. 46, with illustration.
J. Tymms, *Handbook of Bury St. Edmunds* (1905, 8th ed. London. Out of print), pp. 118–121.
Suffolk Instit. of Arch. and Nat. Hist. Proc. x (1900), p. 233, illustrated.
N. Lloyd, p. 328, illustration.

SURREY : FARNHAM CASTLE HALL.

The hall is the centre of the S. block of domestic buildings. It was originally aisled and built by Henry of Blois, Bishop of Winchester (1129–1171). Ancient features include a timber scalloped capital (of the destroyed S. arcade), concealed in a cupboard, and an E. doorway leading to the kitchen and flanked by two smaller openings, partially blocked. Unlike the latter the central doorway opens inwards, and has internal decoration, including a segmental roll-moulded arch and jamb-shafts with 'palm-leaf'

[1] Dr. Margoliouth, '*The Vestiges of the Historic Anglo-Hebrews of East Anglia.*' Certainly the subvault is unnecessarily lofty for a place of storage, and traces of a further range to the W. might be said to fit in with his view that the whole side of the market place was filled by the synagogue and its subsidiary buildings, seminary, baptisteries, and official residences.

[2] *Chronica Jocelini de Brakelonda*, Camden Soc. 1840, p. 33.

[3] *ibid*, p. 56.

capitals ; it is curiously elaborate for a service doorway, being more like an entrance in treatment, while the ornament suggests an addition after the death of Bishop Henry. There are traces of external arcading on the S. wall of the hall.

References : *V.C.H. Surrey* ii (1911), pp. 599–602. Illustrations and coloured plan by Sir Charles Peers.

SUSSEX : NY(E)TIMBER, PAGHAM—BARTON OR MANOR FARM.

The house is reached from a drive near the Lamb Inn. Original features consist of a square building containing N. and S. doorways. Additions include modern rooms connecting the 'aula' with a thirteenth-century chapel. A moat surrounds the site. It has been claimed that the doorways are not rebated, and that the house is thus pre-Conquest. But the recent attribution of herring-bone masonry, which exists here, to the early Norman not Saxon period, puts the building somewhere at the end of the eleventh century. Also an inner rebate to the S. doorway is suggested by the fact that the outer arch is 6 in. wider (and 4 in. higher) than the inner, so that probably the door opened externally to a timber out-building, not now extant. The doorway is blocked, and only the voussoirs can be seen outside, the rest of the wall being rough-cast. Inside, however, the S. wall is visible behind apparent cupboard-doors. The N. doorway is altered.

Condition : Much disguised.

Reference : *Sussex Arch. Collections* xlvi (1903), pp. 115–151, with plan and illustration. H. L. Guermonprez and P. M. Johnston.

SUSSEX : PORTSLADE—MANOR HOUSE RUINS.

The manor-house adjoins the churchyard on the N. Access to the rest of the building is obtained from the Convent of St. Marye, in the gardens of which the ruins stand. The house was built of flint, c. 1150, and contained a first-floor hall. Original features comprise two early two-light windows, of which the S. one has a plain mullion, and the E. a mid-shaft with cushion capital, also a moulded rear-arch. The E. and S. walls alone survive to any extent ; there are also fragments of a later wing projecting W, and making with the hall an L-shaped type of plan.

Condition : The house is a ruin, but its windows are in good condition.

Reference : *Sussex Arch. Collections*, lxxv (1934), pp. 1–18, with plan and measured drawings. A. B. Packham.

SUSSEX : WEST DEAN, NEAR SEAFORD—CHARLESTON MANOR HOUSE.

The manor-house contains a first-floor hall, built c. 1180. It has flint walls with Caen stone dressings, and a good five-shafted two-light window has recently been unblocked in the N. wall.

Reference : *Sussex Notes and Queries*, vol. iv, no. 2 (May 1932). Description, plan and illustrations by W. H. Godfrey.

WILTSHIRE: DEVIZES CASTLE HALL.

This is hardly extant but has been planned. It was 74 ft. by 40 ft. in area, vaulted and probably carried a wooden superstructure. There was a further apartment to the S. (19 ft. by 16 ft.). The castle was built by Bishop Roger of Sarum (1102–1139).

Reference : E. H. Stone, *Devizes Castle* (1920), pp. 26, 115, plan.

WILTSHIRE: CLARENDON PALACE.

Excavations are in progress here under the direction of Dr. Tancred Borenius and Mr. John Charlton. The palace was the scene of the enactment of the Constitutions of Clarendon in 1164 and the Assize of 1166.

Reference : *Antiq. Journal*, xvi (1936), pp. 55–84, with plan.

WORCESTERSHIRE: REDMARLEY D'ABITÔT—BURY FARM.

Bury farm includes a twelfth-century hall built of sandstone. Original features are found only in the basement which has a ribbed vault in three bays, and moulded corbels, a doorway and small one-light windows. The floor is of rammed earth.

Reference : *V.C.H. Worcs.* (1913), p. 482, plan and photographs.

YORKSHIRE: RICHMOND CASTLE—SCOLLAND'S HALL.

Scolland's Hall is situated against the castle wall at the SE. angle. It dates from the late eleventh century except for the S. wall at first-floor level which was rebuilt in the late twelfth century, with the earlier windows probably re-used. Original features include, in the hall, two-light windows and a doorway with jamb-shafts and Corinthianesque capitals ; in the basement loops on the S. wall. The upper floor has gone but joist holes remain showing how little the builders cared for the parallel, the beams apparently slanting across the building as in William II's hall at Westminster. There is a newel stair partially blocked in the NW. angle, and remains of a twelfth-century corbel table on the S. wall. Some herring-bone masonry occurs in the N. and W. walls. The external hall staircase has been destroyed, but some twelfth-century foundations remain ; these probably belonged not to a porch but to a masonry-base for the stair, the latter view being supported by the way in which the staircase is depicted in the fourteenth-century Register of the Honour of Richmond. To the W. are offices built in the early twelfth-century and to the E. an original solar much altered in the thirteenth century.

The hall was probably built by Alan, Earl of Brittany (1071-1089), but was apparently named after Scolland, Lord of Bedale, seneschal to a later Earl Alan (1137–1146).

Condition : Good, except that the roof has gone and many of the windows have lost their mid-shafts. The castle is now in the care of H.M. Office of Works.

References : *H.M.O.W. Official Guide* (1926), with ground plan. *V.C.H. N. Riding* i (1914), pp. 12–16, with first-floor plan. A. Hamilton Thompson, *Military Architecture*, pp. 104, 189.

YORKSHIRE: BURTON AGNES OLD MANOR HOUSE

The Old Hall lies immediately west of its successor, the Jacobean Burton Agnes Hall, between it and the church. When the new hall was built, 1601–10, the old hall apparently was degraded to the status of service quarters, and in the late seventeenth or early eighteenth century became the laundry, the twelfth-century work being then concealed on the outside by a skin of brick on the east and south, either because these walls were the most decayed or because they were most visible from the main house and grounds. The brickwork may date from 1712, to judge from an inscribed stone inside the NE. wall of the hall. Some authorities, however, would date it earlier, in the seventeenth century, with the upper storey added in the eighteenth century, when the present windows were inserted. Certainly this façade with its sash windows forms a complete disguise, and it is with amazement that the visitor, on entering, finds himself in a splendid Norman undercroft.

The most striking twelfth-century features are seen in this undercroft (40 ft. 6 in. by 19 ft. 9 in.), which consists of two aisles of four quadripartite bays divided by cylindrical piers. These three columns have square abaci and water-leaf capitals and annulets: the bases have a roll and hollow with leaf spurs on a square chamfered plinth. The E. and W. responds are half columns of similar design. The transverse, longitudinal and diagonal ribs are semi-circular (or elliptical) and chamfered, with small chalk voussoirs, and chalk filling; many of these voussoirs were so badly decayed that they have had to be replaced with plastic stone. On the lateral walls (N. and S.), the ribs spring from corbels square and chamfered, with smaller ones at the angles; of these the SE. (behind the door) has a carved head of a man with hair in a triple fringe. The corresponding corbel in the NE. angle is modern, for the whole of the NE. bay of the vault is a complete reconstruction, the original having been destroyed in the 'laundry period' to make room for a flight of stairs. On the western pillar there is a set of holes corresponding to the game of Nine Mens' Morris, in which pegs must have been used.

The brick doorway in the S. wall is a repair, but probably on the site of the original basement entrance. The windows on this wall now have sashes. In the N. wall is the only loop window remaining in anything like its original form, with pointed head, splayed to a round rear-arch as it meets the vault; only the E. jamb and head of the loop are original. At the NW. angle a newel staircase rises to the hall; of its doorway part of the soffit remains.

The Hall (44 ft. 9 in. by 22 ft. 6 in.) has been brought back to the proportions it had in the fifteenth century. In the twelfth century the side walls were lower and the pitch of the roof steeper. In the fifteenth century the walls were raised and the existing low-pitched king-post roof erected. Then in the early eighteenth century an additional floor was inserted with a wooden staircase leading up to it in the NE. corner. The windows at first-floor level were completely re-modelled, and an extra tier of windows introduced to light the new storey. The added floor and staircase have been removed, but the windows remain.

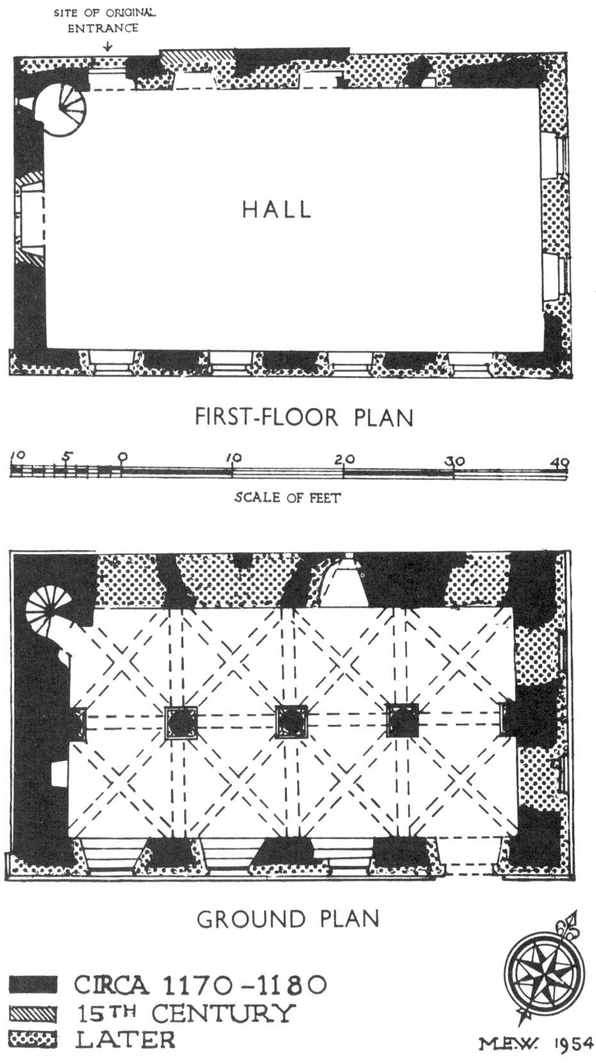

FIG. 13. BURTON AGNES OLD HALL

In the W. wall there was probably a central twelfth-century window, which was replaced in the fifteenth century by a larger and traceried one of which the two-centred arch remains clearly inserted in older masonry. Later, perhaps in the seventeenth century, the traceried head was blocked except for a pair of inserted square chamfered lights, and the sill cut down to form a doorway. On this wall the large masonry of the Norman period can be easily distinguished from the smaller stonework of the upper part of the wall, apparently of the date of the fifteenth-century windows. Near the NW. angle is an original loop, lighting the spiral staircase as it emerges into the hall; there are signs suggesting that this staircase went on up to the roof, and was enclosed. Next to the staircase, in the N. wall, are the remains of the original entrance doorway to the hall, now blocked. The three surviving voussoirs and the top jamb-stone are original; the other jamb-stones are plastic replacements of decayed originals. Towards the eastern end of the wall there is the splayed jamb and half-arch (rounded) of what was probably an original window, also blocked externally.

Condition : Good, since 1948 in the care of the Ministry of Works and restored.

Reference : *M.O.W.* guide (Margaret Wood, 1956), with ground and first-floor plans from which the above description was obtained.

YORKSHIRE: FOUNTAINS ABBEY—GUEST-HOUSES

We can learn a great deal about medieval houses from monastic architecture, for here may be preserved certain domestic features lost to us elsewhere. This is the case at Fountains Abbey where there are two separate and adjoining guest-houses built after the fire of 1147, the eastern probably first. They contain first-floor halls above a once vaulted basement divided into two aisles by a central row of pillars, the eastern (73 ft. by 23 ft. 3 in.) of 6 double bays, the western (49 ft. 3 in. by 24 ft. 9 in.) of 4. Many windows of single or double lights remain, including blocked circular ones in the gables. But the most interesting feature is the clever planning of the garderobe projections over the stream, to serve both floors of the buildings.

Reference : *Yorks. Archaeological Journal,* xv (1900), pp. 120–5, fig. 26 — W. H. St. John Hope.
F. H. Crossley, *The English Abbey* (1935). Plan by J. Arthur Reeve in cover. Photographs by the late Professor U. T. Holmes of N. Carolina (1959) to whom the author is greatly indebted for his kind advice and help.

YORKSHIRE: WHARRAM PERCY: EAST RIDING. SE/858646.
NORMAN MANOR HOUSE.

In the work on the deserted medieval village by J. G. Hurst and M. W. Beresford, the undercroft of a Norman manor house was excavated. It is built of chalk blocks with sandstone dressings and measures 38 ft. by 17 ft. 6 in. internally, with walls 4 ft. thick (compared with 5 ft. at Burton Agnes). A row of three central pillar bases has been found; these presumably held timber supports as no sign of vaulting was discovered. In the roof, tiles seem to have been used round the chimney, and thatch elsewhere.

From a waterleaf capital and waterholding base from the fireplace above, E. A. Gee gives a date c. 1180–90. This fits in with the payments in the Pipe Roll which suggest that building was in progress between 1177 and 1196.

Reference : *Medieval Archaeology*, I (1957), pp. 162, 164; II (1958), pp. 205–7, fig. 51, plan; III (1959), pp. 318–19; V (1961), p. 338; VI–VII (1962–3), pp. 146–7.

YORKSHIRE: YORK—THE NORMAN HOUSE.

Part of a house c. 1170–80 stands in an alley off the Stonegate. It was discovered in 1939 during demolition work in Church Passage, being previously hidden by a brick outer wall. The chief feature is a window of two round-headed lights with foliated capital to the mullion and a semi-circular rear arch; it presumably lit a first-floor hall or solar. In the adjoining wall is a rectangular cupboard; these features, together with the masonry in squared blocks, resembling the mid twelfth-century 'King John's House' at Southampton.

PEMBROKESHIRE: MANORBIER CASTLE.

The domestic range is an untouched example of early medieval accommodation, and shows the improvement of comfort and privacy from the late twelfth to the thirteenth centuries. Although in Pembrokeshire, 'the little England beyond Wales', it had a Norman owner, and may be used to illustrate a development which has been altered by modernization in many English castles. Against the SW. curtain a first-floor hall was constructed, with external staircase and adjoining butteries, over which the solar, with end fireplace, occupied the second floor. We thus have an 'end hall' with solar-service block, all raised on semi-circular barrel vaults suggesting a date in the latter part of the twelfth century. This building was probably seen by the chronicler Giraldus Cambrensis, born here c. 1146, traditionally in the round tower at the eastern angle of the castle enclosure, though this tower would seem not earlier than 1200.

About 1260 a second solar was added to the opposite end of the hall, in a cross-wing; and off one outer angle of it is the vestibule to a chapel, and off the other, towards the curtain, the passage to a garderobe built over the moat. The chapel is also reached from the court by an external staircase.

Reference : *Royal Archaeological Institute Programme of Summer Meeting at Tenby*, 1962, p. 21 (sketch plan).

FURTHER NOTES

DURHAM: WASHINGTON OLD HALL (National Trust).

This Jacobean building incorporates parts of the manor house, c. 1183.

HAMPSHIRE: HAMBLEDON—ROOKWOOD FARM.

The round arches to two opposite first-floor hall windows remain; the south with chamfered hood having inturned impost ends, the north with inner arch as well, and semi-circular rear arch.

ISLE OF WIGHT: CALBOURNE—SWAINSTONE HALL.

This is a thirteenth-century hall with a late twelfth-century annexe.

Reference: *V.C.H. Hants*, v (1912), p. 217 (plan).

KENT: CANTERBURY—GUILDHALL SITE.

On the site of the Guildhall, in the street of that name, there is a tall column with scalloped capital and square abacus, of c. 1180. It has above it the start of keel-moulded ribs rising steeply and suggesting a lofty undercroft of which it was the central feature, like that in the keep at Newcastle (1172–7).

KENT: CANTERBURY—36 HIGH STREET—'THE MINT'.

The twelfth-century undercroft was probably the Mint, and there remains one aisle of a subvault of four quadripartite bays, with evidence of a parallel aisle, divided by square piers with scalloped capitals, of which two survive; the diagonals are chamfered but not the transverse arches. It was 44 ft. by 26 ft. originally.

LINCOLNSHIRE: LINCOLN—DELORAINE COURT.

The house is situated in James Street, NW. of the Cathedral Close. It is T-shaped in plan, with the head of the T running N.–S., and a courtyard on the SE. towards the street; it is now divided into three houses. Although outwardly showing seventeenth-century and later features only, it contains three early twelfth-century columns and very thick walling.

The nucleus seems to have been a great hall, lying E.–W. of which thick Norman walls remain. There was apparently a projecting range on the E. at right angles to the hall, rebuilt and extended in the seventeenth century, the date of the entrance porch. In this cross-range the W. wall towards the hall is 3 ft. 6 in. and upwards in thickness.

But the chief interest lies in the W. range, possibly a storage undercroft to the domestic block, lying N.–S. at right angles to the hall, and projecting chiefly S. Apart from the seventeenth-century N. extension, it is of exceptional length (89 ft. 6 in. by 16 ft.) and is divided by a thick wall into two compartments. The northern (37 ft. long) was probably of four double bays, and retains two central columns, partly built up in later walls. The southern room (50 ft. 6 in.) has a free-standing column near the N. end, but others may be hidden by later sub-divisions, and the spacing suggests a room of five bays, unless the northern portion only is original. The three columns have scalloped capital and square abacus, chamfered base and plinth. No sign of the vaulting remains but otherwise there is a resemblance to a monastic western range.

References : *Lincolnshire Notes & Queries*, VI (1901), pp. 161–3. E. Mansel Sympson.
The Lincolnshire Historian, 10 (1952), pp. 356–8. M. E. Wood—plans.

NORTHANTS: BARNACK.

The Norman portions of the manor house have been destroyed.

Reference : Turner & Parker, p. 52 (illustration).
V.C.H. Northants., II (1906), pp. 468, 472.

NORFOLK: NORWICH—MUSIC HOUSE OR ISAAC'S HOUSE—167 KING STREET.

This was built c. 1175, probably by Isaac, the Jewish financier. It has an undercroft in two sections, divided by a stone wall. The eastern (solar) cellar is a groined vault of three bays separated by transverse bands, and having a newel staircase in the NE. angle while the western cellar has the same wide arch between its two bays, but here there are diagonal ribs of a bold roll section flanked by hollow chamfers. Two loop windows remain to the S., and on the same wall is evidence of a forebuilding once containing an external staircase to the hall above. The lower portion of one columned jamb of the entrance remains. The upper part was altered by the Pastons in the late sixteenth century, and a second floor inserted in recent years.

Condition : Good.
References : E. A. Kent: *Norfolk Archaeology*, XXVIII (1945), pp. 28–38 (plan and illustration).
W. Buston: *Country Life* (1942), pp. 360–1 (plan and illustration).

SOMERSET: CHEDDAR PALACE.

In 1960 a palace of the Kings of Wessex was discovered, and before the building of a large new school, the site was excavated by Mr. P. A. Rahtz for the Ministry of Public Buildings and Works, 1961–2.

A great ninth-century hall was uncovered, probably that of King Alfred himself. This 'Long Hall' was a boat-shaped building, rather wider in the middle than at the end, about 78 ft. by 20 ft. and of post and trench construction. In a continuous trench small posts at the outer vertical edge probably had planking in between, while an inner row of posts sloping inwards may have formed struts to support an upper floor. This would be an arrangement unparalleled elsewhere at this date, but fitting in with documentary evidence of the meeting of the Witan in 978 at Calne where the floor collapsed. The hall of the Witan had to be large to accommodate the West Saxon council, with representatives from many areas.

This building was abandoned in the tenth century, probably in the period after 930, which included the reign of Athelstan (925–40), a widely travelled king, who perhaps brought in a new architectural technique from abroad. A chapel, altered later, was built across its site, and a new 'West Hall' constructed further south. This was more rectangular (60 ft. by 28–30 ft.) with doorways at the ends, and an internal porch at the west end. It was again of wood, but with massive posts set in pits at intervals of 8 ft., presumably linked by horizontal timbers into which planks were slotted. This would be the hall in which the Witan met in 941, 956, and 968, and perhaps was the scene of King Edmund's reconciliation with St. Dunstan, after his miraculous escape from death in Cheddar Gorge (941).

The West Hall was made narrower (60 ft. by 24 ft.) in the eleventh century, and again reconstructed in the early twelfth century, with new post-holes. Its wall being in line with the post-holes of the S. arcade of a new East Hall, it was probably contemporary with it.

The East Hall may be the largest timber hall so far known in this country, being 110 ft. by 54 ft. in area, aisled in 10 bays of post and timber slot construction, with arcade posts 2 ft. square, set in large pits 6 ft. deep; this might allow for arcades 50 ft. to 60 ft. high. Across the E. end was the foundation for a gallery or balcony. It dates from the early twelfth century, and was certainly in use when Henry I (1100–35) and Henry II (1154–89) stayed at the palace. Later it was rebuilt with low stone walls and renewed arcade posts (6 bays) and also reduced in length (71 ft. by 48 ft.). This reconstruction probably dates from 1209–11 when King John spent £50 on 'his houses at Cheddar', and had timber (? for the arcade posts) brought from Wales. In 1213, however, on his submission to the Pope, the manor was given to the Bishop of Wells, and in the later thirteenth century the hall was rebuilt in stone without aisles (66 ft. by 42 ft.), with a tripartite addition and garderobe at the E. end.

References : *Medieval Archaeology*, VI–VII (1962–3), pp. 53–66, with plans and illustrations: P. A. Rahtz.

The History of the King's Works: The Middle Ages (1963), pp. 907–9, with coloured plan after Rahtz. R. Allen Brown, H. M. Colvin, and A. J. Taylor.

SUFFOLK: FRAMLINGHAM CASTLE.

There are traces of an original stone house of two storeys, with two chimneys, built by Hugh Bigod c. 1150–60 and thus before the curtain wall of 1190–1200 was built against the outside of it, the original defences being of timber. As the lower storey had a fireplace also, there may have been an upper and a lower hall, or hall with solar above. The cylindrical chimneys have round-headed lancet vents, Tudor brick extensions probably replacing a conical cap.

SUFFOLK: STANSFIELD, NEAR CLARE.

A twelfth-century aisled hall with wooden piers existed here until its destruction in 1928. Two wooden posts are preserved.

SUSSEX: CHICHESTER—VICARS' HALL UNDERCROFT.

Ribs rising vertically over two much lower columns produce a vault 11 ft. 6 in. high, and a double aisle of three quadripartite bays, in a late twelfth-century undercroft, 35 ft. by 25 ft., once serving a guildhall but later incorporated into the Vicars' Hall. It is now a restaurant.

Reference: F. W. Steer: *The Vicars' Hall at Chichester and its Undercroft* (1958).

SUSSEX: NEW SHOREHAM. THE MARLEPINS.

This was possibly a toll house of the de Braoses, lords of Shoreham in the twelfth and thirteenth centuries, where their agent collected taxes and harbour dues.

The front, which has chequer-work of flint and Caen stone, was apparently rebuilt in the early fourteenth century. But the evidence of a Norman window, now doorway, on the east wall, shows that the building dates from the twelfth century. The left-hand south doorway still opens on to the stairs to the upper floor, and the larger right-hand one to the basement, here two feet below street level. Between them is a small 'business window', and there is a larger window, altered, to the floor above.

Reference: *Sussex Archaeological Collections*, LXV (1924), pp. 158–97. A. B. Packham (plans and illustrations).

SUSSEX: OLD ERRINGHAM.

Here there is a small barn which is said to have been the chapel of a manor house.

SUSSEX: SOUTH MALLING.

Here is a portion of wall which probably belonged to a manor house of the Archbishops of Canterbury, and might thus have been the scene of the leaping table which so startled the murderers of Becket. The wall can be seen in the garden of Old Malling Farm.

Norman subvaults partially remain at the Bishops' Palaces at Lincoln and Norwich.

CLASSIFIED LIST OF NORMAN HOUSES WITH APPROXIMATE DATE AND DIMENSIONS.[1]

	Date	Internal Length ft.	Internal Breadth ft.	Width of Wall Ground Floor.	Width of Wall First Floor.
I. First-floor Halls:					
(*a*) *Town Houses*—					
King John's House, Southampton . .	c. 1150	44 –	27½	2′ 10″ (N.)	2′ 2″ (N.)
				3′ 7″ (W.)	2′ 10″ (W.)
Jew's House, Lincoln	1170–80	33½	15	2′ 8″	2′ 8″
Aaron the Jew's House, Lincoln	1170–80	—	—	3′ & 4′, etc.	—
Canute's Palace, Southampton	c. 1180	111	—	2′ 9″	2′ 9″
Moyse's Hall, Bury St. Edmunds . .	c. 1180	44	37½	3′ 8″	3′ 8″
St. Mary's Guild, Lincoln	1180–90	23+	18	4′ 7″	—
(*b*) *Manor Houses*—					
Portslade	c. 1150	32	21½	c. 3′ 9″	c. 3′
Hemingford Grey	c. 1150	31 –	18	—	3′, 3′ 4″, 3′ 5″
Saltford	c. 1150	—	—	c. 3′ –	c. 3′
Charleston	c. 1180	37	18	c. 2′ 6″	c. 2′ 6″
Merton Hall	c. 1200	60	20	2′ 4″–3′ 9″	2′ 6″–3′ 8″
Boothby Pagnell	c. 1200	48½	17½	4′	c. 2′ 9″
(*c*) *Castle Halls*—					
Scolland's Hall, Richmond	Late eleventh and twelfth century	76	26	4′	3′ 4″, 4′
Christchurch	c. 1160	68	24	4′ 4″ (W.)	—
				4′ 11″ (N.S.)	4′ 9″
				5′ 6″ (E.)	5′ 4″
Durham, Pudsey's Hall	c. 1170	145	26+	—	—
Wolvesey Castle, Winchester	c. 1170	134	29½	5′ 4″, etc.	—

[1] The dimensions are approximate as opposite walls often differ in length, and old walls slope, sometimes even out of the parallel—(e.g. Jew's House and Aaron's House). For clarity, length and breadth measurements are given to the nearest 6 in.

	Date	Internal Length Ft.	Internal Breadth Ft.	Width of Wall Ground Floor.	Width of Wall First Floor.
II. GROUND FLOOR HALLS, AISLED :					
Westminster Hall	Late eleventh and fourteenth century	239½	67½	—	—
Leicester Castle Hall	c. 1150	76	51	4¼′	—
Hereford, Great Hall of the Bishops ..	c. 1150	—	—	—	—
Farnham Castle Hall[1] (Capital c. 1150) E. Doorway	c. 1190	65	43	—	—
Oakham Castle Hall[2]	c. 1190	66	44	2′ 10″ and 3′ 6″	—
Bristol	1200+	—	—	—	—
III. GROUND FLOOR HALLS, UNAISLED :					
Minster Court (N. Range)	c. 1120	63	26½	3′ 6″, 4′ and 4′ 3″	—
Horton Court	c. 1140	31	16	2′ 6″+ (N. & S.) 4′ 3″ (W.)	—
Sutton Courtenay, ‘ Norman Hall ’ ..	c. 1190	50	17	2′ 8″	—
Appleton Manor	c. 1210	38½	24½	2′ 6″, 2′ 9″ and 3′ 1″	—

[1] Width of Nave, 27 ft. ; Aisles, 8½ ft.
[2] Width of Nave, 20 ft. ; Aisles, 9 ft. (piers 2 ft. in diameter).

	Date	INTERNAL Length Ft.	INTERNAL Breadth Ft.	WIDTH OF WALL Ground Floor.	WIDTH OF WALL First Floor.
IV. PALACES:					
Sherborne Castle (First-floor hall)	c. 1135 or later	68	20	—	—
Wolvesey Castle	—	—	—	—	—
Bishop's Waltham Palace	—	—	—	—	—
Clarendon Palace (aisled hall)	Late twelfth-century	83	51	—	—
V. SUBVAULTS:					
St. Thomas Street, Winchester	twelfth century	27	17½	c. 4′ 4″	—
Redmarley d'Abitot, Bury Farm (no original features in first-floor hall above)	late twelfth century	30	18	c. 3′ 5″	—
Southampton, vault on Western Shore ..	late twelfth century	56	19½	8′ 8″ (W.)	—
VI. EXAMPLES OF UNCERTAIN TYPE:					
Barton or Manor Farm, Nytimber	late eleventh century	19	17	2′ 10″	—
Early Hall at Chilham Castle	late eleventh century	30	19½	under 3′ 6″	—
West Malling, Prebendal House, ? Solar[1] ..	c. 1140–50	29½	14	2′ 6″	1′ 10″
Stamford, 'Norman House'	c. 1150	—	—	—	—

[1] Measurements through the courtesy of Mr. Elliston-Erwood, F.S.A.

	Date	Internal Length Ft.	Internal Breadth Ft.	Width of Wall Ground Floor.	Width of Wall First Floor.
VII. Examples of Uncertain Date:					
Jew's Court	—	27	20	2′ 11″	2′ 4″ & 2′ 2″
Luddesdown Court	—	—	—	c. 3′–	—
Exeter, house in Preston Street	—	28	19	—	—
VIII. Examples not Extant but Illustrated:					
Southampton, house in St. Michael's Square	—	50	20	—	—
Smaller house in Blue Anchor Lane ..	—	45	20	—	—
London, Crypts of the Priors of Lewes, Southwark	—	I 40½	16½	—	—
	—	31	14–	—	—
	—	39	18	—	—
	—	II 26	21	—	—
London, Corbet Court	—	c. 40′ square		—	—

DATE

With very few exceptions surviving Norman houses date to the second half of the twelfth century ; Scolland's Hall and West Malling, Minster Horton and Nytimber being at present the only earlier examples. This late twelfth-century date may be fortuitous : it would be natural to expect later buildings to be more abundant ; but such a preponderance of evidence on one side calls for another explanation.

Some would attribute it to the fact that earlier stone dwelling-houses never existed, castles forming the only Norman type until the reign of Henry II. Our earlier examples oppose this view : nevertheless it is partially correct. The Normans on their arrival in England would be more likely to build castles than manor houses, so as to keep and emphasise a predominence not accompanied by superiority in numbers. The early twelfth century saw Henry I's work in the direction of wealth and order overturned by the Anarchy which followed his death in 1135, and it was not until the reign of his grandson that richer and more settled conditions encouraged the building of structures which were neither castles nor hovels.[1]

But more significant is a second reason for the late date of surviving stone houses : the fact that until the reign of Henry II stone was not in general use for building, even castles being mainly composed of timber.[2] These latter would be the first to be translated into the less destructible material. Thus if many early twelfth-century dwelling-houses existed, they would be of wood, and so do not survive.

Even under Henry II the question of defence was important and it was safer to have the living-rooms raised to first-floor level,[3] a similar arrangement being found in the keeps of twelfth-century castles. In the thirteenth century conditions were still more secure, and the hall tended to come downstairs. Yet first-floor halls were still built, such as Little Wenham

[1] Yet Horton (c. 1140) dates from this period, and perhaps West Malling (c. 1140–50).

[2] There are exceptions, such as Richmond, in areas where stone was expecially abundant and easily worked.

[3] The aisled hall is not here considered.

Hall, Suffolk, and this century with the fourteenth may be considered a period of transition. It was not until the fifteenth century that the ground-floor hall was usual.

TYPES OF NORMAN HOUSE

There are three main types to be found in surviving Norman houses, the first-floor hall, the aisled hall on ground level, and the unaisled ground-floor hall.

Although we should expect a difference in type between town and manor houses, occasioned by considerations of space, it is noteworthy that the compact first-floor hall is common to both. No doubt, however, the number of outbuildings, probably timber-built, would be greater in the country. In both the stone hall is raised on a basement[1] either vaulted as at Moyse's Hall and Boothby Pagnell, or with a wooden ceiling as apparently existed at Jew's House and Charleston Manor. Such an arrangement would provide storage accommodation below, and raise the living-rooms to a defensible height above the ground. Thus the hall windows could be larger, loops sufficing for the basement.

This type is also found in castles, where a hall was often built apart from the keep, and formed a separate house in the bailey, usually against the curtain, where an escarpment or other feature gave it the most protection. At Richmond and Christchurch these halls are distinct buildings, and can be classed as Norman houses. Other castle halls on the first-floor occur at Durham[2] and Wolvesey Castle, Winchester, but here they form an integral part of the general plan.

But other castle halls seem to have been aisled,[3] and were thus built at ground-level, where the solid

[1] The term 'cellar' is used as an alternative for basement in the medieval period. Both words have now an underground sense, but here they will be used, unless otherwise indicated, for rooms, generally for storage, on ground level.

[2] Bishop Pudsey's range, the upper part of which is called Constable's Hall. The 'Great Hall' is of thirteenth-century build.

[3] Winchester Castle Hall, Bishop Auckland (now a chapel), Ashby-de-la-Zouch, Warkworth. See Clapham and Godfrey, p. 73.

earth could serve as a platform for the piers. Indeed, the aisled hall seems to have been the chief type in the twelfth century for a hall of any width, as long timbers were not easily obtainable, and arcades, dividing up the span into shorter sections, simplified the problem of roofing.[1] This was solved in the fourteenth century by the introduction of the hammer-beam roof, a method of construction based on a series of superimposed brackets in turn supported and supporting in a step fashion akin to the corbelled vaults of antiquity. It not only dispensed with the tie-beam, but made unnecessary the division of a large compartment into nave and aisles. Even before this the aisled hall was passing out of favour, and at the end of the fourteenth century the greatest of the Norman halls of this kind, that at Westminster, was remodelled, and a splendid hammer-beam roof replaced the old triple arrangement. Thereafter there are only isolated examples, such as the fifteenth-century Guildhall at York, but the type persisted into modern times in the form of barns.

Ground-floor halls without aisles do exist, but it is noteworthy that they are either doubtfully domestic or doubtfully Romanesque. There are four of them so far known, Horton and Minster Courts which date to the first half of the twelfth century, Sutton Courtenay ' Norman Hall ' (c. 1190) and Appleton Manor (c. 1210). It will be advisable to judge each example on its merits.

With regard to a domestic character, Minster is the most dubious—the hall appearing to form part of a semi-monastic plan comprising a church and dormitory, or if domestic it is of a most unusual type of Norman house.

Appleton can also be dismissed, this time on grounds of date : it belongs to the first quarter of the thirteenth century, and will be considered as a type of transition into the normal medieval house plan.

Horton and Sutton Courtenay have been called chapels, the latter by several authorities. This may

[1] Aisled halls were usually built of wood, and so more cheaply.

be part of a certain timidity to recognise a Norman house as such from which the first-floor hall by its very character is exempt.[1] Both houses are rightly orientated and have north and south doorways towards the western angles of the building: these doors are opposite at Horton but not quite facing at Sutton Courtenay.

Like Sutton Courtenay the fact that Horton Court is near the church is an argument in favour of its being a Norman house. The church of St. James, a few yards away, was rebuilt in the fourteenth and early fifteenth centuries, but presumably on the site of an earlier church which in the twelfth century was given as a prebend to Sarum. Horton Court is said to be the prebendal manor house, and the position of its north doorway in direct line with the priest's door in the chancel lends colour to the supposition.

Thus we cannot neglect the existence of unaisled halls on the ground-floor in the twelfth century, though the evidence suggests that they were uncommon in stone. There are several reasons that might be given for their occurrence. Some might even attribute them to monastic influence, through the resemblance of Sutton Courtenay and the semi-monastic Minster to a common type of frater of which a good example exists at Dover, and indeed bears a strong likeness to the hall at Minster. The windows are high on the walls not only for defence but to carry the draughts from unglazed windows over the heads of the occupants. In early halls light was an advantage tempered by the entry of wind and rain, for shutters kept out all three together. Later in the Middle Ages safer conditions and the use of glass brought the windows nearer to ground level.

Another view might be that these halls are the translation of wooden houses into stone. This involves, however, a consideration of the material used in the first-floor type of hall. All surviving examples of the latter are in stone, but it may be that in some, stone was used only in the basement to protect valuable or

[1] Yet at least one of the latter has been called a synagogue.

inflammable stores against fire; the less expensive hall above could be replaced more easily. No examples of this kind exist, but there is a possibility that the castle hall at Devizes was of such a composite build. The subvault that remains at St. Thomas Street, Winchester, may have carried an upper floor of timber, also the London crypt, now destroyed, at Corbet Court and those of the Priors of Lewes in Southwark. A complete first-floor hall in wood is unlikely, for there would be no advantage and only danger in an elevated position when the basement could easily be set alight. Not only would the latter lose its purpose as a safe place for storage, but the fact that the hall was raised above it make egress difficult in case of fire. If the wooden stairs were burnt the occupants could only escape by jumping from the doors and windows.[1] It is thus probable that the most common type of house in the twelfth century, the house of timber now destroyed, would have its living-rooms on the ground-floor with possibly other sleeping accomodation in a loft in the roof above. Aisles would not be necessary save in the larger buildings. Sometimes such an arrangement may have been translated into the more durable material, which would explain the stone examples left to us, but it is more probable that where stone could be afforded, the builder would choose the compact defensible first-floor hall. That is what the available evidence suggests, and the stone hall on ground level seems to have been a matter of special circumstances or of individual caprice.

Again it might be argued that in such unaisled ground-floor halls we have prototypes of the typical medieval house. But it will be well to postpone the discussion as to which type of Norman house survived, and first consider the plan of each and their component parts.

Plan.

It is not possible to recover a complete plan of the Norman house owing to the fragmentary state of most

[1] At any level two-light windows do not provide a pleasant means of egress.

existing examples, and the non-survival of wooden outbuildings which probably housed the offices and almost certainly the kitchen. With regard to the main building, the plan is generally oblong, though the corners are rarely true right angles.

(1) *The first-floor hall.*—The first-floor hall occurs in two main types: (a) the single compartment plan, and (b) the hall and solar plan. This classification is based on the surviving stone walls, and does not take account of possible timber sub-divisions and additions. Also the varieties of basement are considered elsewhere.

(*a*) *The single compartment plan* is found in Jew's House, Hemingford Grey and Charleston manor houses, and probably at Canute's Palace, Southampton. The solar at Merton Hall, Cambridge, is a thirteenth-century addition to this type of house, and Christchurch castle hall will also count as an example, although there used to be traces of adjoining buildings, possibly somewhat similar to the arrangement at Richmond.

(*b*) *The hall and solar plan*[1] is less usual. It occurs certainly at Boothby Pagnell, where the solar is added at one end of an ordinary single apartment of the same build; and at Moyse's Hall where a third apartment may have existed but is now destroyed. In these the separate rooms are all in a line forming one building block, and in the case of Boothby Pagnell probably covered by a single roof. King John's House seems to have been of this type.

The hall and solar arrangement is probably a typological development from the single-compartment plan, in which the upper end of the hall was no doubt divided off in some cases to serve as a private bed-chamber for the lord and lady. The lower end may also have been partitioned to form a passage sheltering the body of the hall from draughts when the entrance door was opened. Curtains probably were sometimes used for the purpose, and perhaps the upper end was

[1] The 'solar' often called the 'chamber' was the private bed-chamber of the lord and lady and was always on the first-floor. The word 'solar,' 'soller,' or 'solarium' is also used in the general sense of a room above ground-floor level. For other uses of the word see Hamilton Thompson, p. 192.

only separated from the hall at night when the lord and his family retired.[1]

Both types of hall may be classed together with regard to the arrangement of doors, fireplaces and windows.

The entrance doorway was generally placed in one of the side walls at the lower end of the hall. The high table would thus be as far from the door as possible. Instances of an entrance in this position are found at Jew's House, Christchurch, and Boothby Pagnell, though sometimes, as at Merton Hall and Hemingford Grey, the doorway is placed in the end wall, a situation unusual in a medieval house.

The wall fireplace commonly occurs near the middle of the side wall opposite to that containing the entrance. This is the arrangement at the five houses mentioned, in which the original plan is most easily recoverable.

All the windows never survive in any house, but they seem to have been distributed at fairly regular intervals, one in the end, two or three in the side walls. At Christchurch the north window has especially elaborate decoration, and indicates the upper end of the hall. Smaller windows occur in the gables.

An unusual arrangement is found in Jew's House and Aaron's House, Lincoln. Here the main entrance is on the ground-floor near the centre of the side wall facing the street, and a first-floor fireplace buttress is supported on the hood-mould of the doorway. This neat arrangement was possibly designed to do away with the necessity of an outside stair, at least on the street front.[2] But it may be that the ground-floor entrance was adopted as being safer, and indeed this might be used as evidence that Jews, fearing persecution, actually built these two houses.

Usually, however, the basement doorway is plain ; and in an undivided cellar, occurs at the end of one

[1] A somewhat similar use of curtains is found in an illustration of a Saxon house (Harleian MSS. no. 603, fol. 67). Illustration in Lloyd, p. 5.

[2] In the thirteenth - century Hundred Rolls, there are complaints of encroachments on the public way by external staircases. S. O. Addy, *Evolution of the English House* (1933), p. 111.

of the side walls, sometimes on the same wall as the first-floor entrance, but at the other end. Loops were apparently the usual form of windows, but unfortunately evidence of their arrangement only remains in castle halls. At Richmond and Christchurch the outer wall of castle and hall are the same, and the loops naturally occur here, while the doorway is opposite. King John's House apparently had several large arches on the western wall, and this suggests a use for the transference of merchandise on to the quay.

(2) *The Aisled Hall.* Oakham is the only good example of the arrangement in an aisled hall. The entrance occurred originally in a similar position to that which it occupied in the first-floor hall, namely at the end of one of the side walls. In the end wall near it are blocked doorways leading to the offices in outbuildings now destroyed. Above is a first-floor doorway apparently approached by an internal stairway, possibly resting on the curious projection remaining on the north wall. This doorway is also blocked, but apparently led to an apartment above the offices.

At Farnham the entrance was in the normal position but has been replaced, and three service doorways survive in the end wall. The elaborate central one opens inwards, and flanking it are smaller doorways opening outwards as at Oakham.

(3) *Ground-floor halls without aisles.* Of ground-floor halls Appleton has a similar arrangement to Oakham, but with originally another door opposite the entrance.[1] Here the service doorways are two in number, and unblocked.[2] This example, however, belongs rather to the Early English period ; earlier halls at Horton and Sutton Courtenay show opposite doorways near the lower end of the side walls, but no visible openings in the end wall.

There is no evidence of a wall fireplace in any ground-floor hall, whether aisled or unaisled, but the

[1] D. and S. Lyson, *Magna Britannia* (1806), i, 212. The position is now occupied by a modern window.

[2] These probably led into pantry and buttery in a wooden building with a solar on the first floor. There is no sign of a stone annexe save for a later medieval wall and traces of a newel stair.

windows are at a lower level in the aisled hall, this being occasioned by the construction of the roof.

BUILDING MATERIAL

The Norman houses that remain to us are of stone or flint, although no doubt wood was more often used in manor and town houses, and with clay and wattle was probably the sole material for the houses of the poor.[1] Even in twelfth-century London the majority of the houses were wooden, with thatched roofs, and thus fires were frequent. The Building Regulations of 1189[2] offered special privileges to citizens who would build in stone and roof with tile, but this seems to have had little effect; and if timber were used, stone party walls 3 ft. thick and 16 ft. high were to divide one house from another. The use of wood seems to have persisted, however, and a stone house denoted position and means, probably even in districts where, unlike the Home Counties, stone was quarried locally. Nevertheless there must have been many more stone houses than the few survivors suggest: for instance, we know there were others besides Moyse's Hall at Bury St. Edmunds.

For the aisled hall, the construction of which was in origin one of timber, wood doubtless remained the chief material in the twelfth century, translations into stone such as the hall at Oakham being exceptional. We have documentary evidence of such a timber hall, now destroyed, in the castles of Hertford and Pleshy, and the hall of the Bishops of Hereford, although now disguised, is an example yet remaining. These timber halls probably had a rubble base, as at Hereford, on which the half-timber walls would rest, and the type of hall at Leicester Castle, where a complete shell of stone encloses the wooden arcading, may be a development from this.

[1] Evidence for the flimsy nature of the houses of the ordinary man is found in the *London Assize* of 1212, which orders their removal if on fire by hook and cord. The *Assize of Clarendon* (1166) enacts that any person who harbours a heretic shall have his house carried outside the town and burnt. (Article 21.)

[2] See Turner and Parker, Appendix i, p. 275 *et seq.* for the *London Assize* of 1189 from the '*Liber de Antiquis Legibus.*'

The stone used would depend in most cases on local conditions, for transport from any distance was expensive. Some of the best stone houses lie on the limestone strip which runs diagonally across England from Lincoln to Somerset, fringed by parallel belts of lias, inferior to the oolite but still good building material. Outliers of the limestone are found in the Isle of Purbeck, also in the Isle of Wight, whence it was easily transported to Southampton by sea. In fact, conveyance by water was quicker and cheaper than by land when the only good roads were those made by the Romans a thousand years before. For this reason Caen stone from Normandy was frequently used in Medieval England, and is found in the dressings at Charleston and Nytimber. Sandstones are quarried in the West Midlands, but few houses remain of this material. The East and South East are poor in building-stone, and in the Norman period, brick other than reused Roman work, does not appear. Flint, however, found underneath the chalk, was an adequate substitute, also clunch (hardened chalk) and Kentish rag, a local stone not easily worked.

Good ashlar workmanship is found, and a few houses are entirely built of such masonry.[1] Most however have walls of coursed or random rubble, or flint, with the dressings only of cut stone. Ashlar quoins are usual, normally arranged in pseudo ‘long-and-short’ work, which however is not characteristic of the Norman period alone. Sometimes the angle is chamfered. Shallow plinths also occur.

Herringbone masonry is a characteristic of early Norman, not Saxon work,[2] and can be seen in the walls at Minster (west range), Richmond and Nytimber.

Buttresses

The usual type is the flat or pilaster buttress of shallow projection, continuing the height of two storeys, but sometimes narrowing above the string marking first-floor level. The stepped buttress with

[1] Probably with a rubble core.

[2] A. W. Clapham, *English Romanesque Architecture after the Conquest*, p. 115.

weathered offsets indicates transition into the Early English type, when the thicker buttress counteracted the thinning of the walls. The Norman buttresses, however, are often decorative, as the thick walls are usually adequate in themselves to support a vaulted undercroft. The chimney buttress is described elsewhere.

Width of Walls[1]

Domestic architecture does not bear out the current view that Norman walls are always over 3 ft. in width. Even ground-floor widths occur under 3 ft. where the cellar is unvaulted, with measurements from 2 ft. 6 in. to 2 ft. 11 in. Under 2 ft. 6 in. is rare, however. Basement walls of 3 ft. to 4 ft. and even over are found, and especially when the ground-floor is vaulted. First-floor walls often thin from 3 in. to 9 in. to provide a ledge for the floor joists. At King John's House, the north wall thins to 2 ft. 2 in. However, such slight walls are rare, and the usual width is from 2 ft. 8 in. to 3 ft. 6 in.

VAULTING

The basement of the first-floor hall was often vaulted, and three varieties are found of the semicircular vault: the barrel vault, which is least popular; the groined vault; and the ribbed vault. The quadripartite plan is general, also the chamfered rib.

ROOFS

No original roofs exist save for a few fragments at Hereford and possibly at Leicester, but we have evidence of their pitch from gables surviving at Oakham, Saltford and Christchurch. This seems to have been steep, on the average 55°–60°, but Mr. Fosbrooke's reconstruction of Leicester Hall gives an angle of c. 45°. However, here the roof had to cover a wide span of nave and aisles together, while at

[1] For details, see Classified List.

Oakham[1] the three parts had each a separate roof, and but for the absence of clerestorey windows, this hall might be called basilican.

An open timber roof is probable, even for the first-floor hall, where all attic floors are later insertions. Possibly this was a cruder form of the later tie-beam and king-post roof, or of the arch-braced collar-beam type so popular in the thirteenth and fourteenth centuries. The stone corbels still *in situ* at Christchurch and Durham may have supported braces to the collar beam, or wall-posts stiffening a simple coupled-rafter roof.

Roof-coverings

As no Norman roofs survive externally, there is naturally no direct evidence of their covering, and we are forced to use documentary evidence alone.

Thatch is mentioned in the London Assize of 1212,[2] when citizens were urged to whitewash it as a precaution against fire. Thick tiles were recommended as being safer, and Jocelin de Brakelond records how Abbot Samson ordered the replacement of reeds by slates for the roofs of the monastic stables and offices also to lessen the danger of fire.[3]

In twelfth-century illustrations of churches, the roofs are often covered with curved tiles resembling the Roman imbrices, and in the earlier Harleian MSS.[4] Saxon houses are portrayed as combining various methods of roofing, and having not only these semicircular tiles, but also flat square shingles, also oval shingles resembling Norman scale ornament.[5]

[1] In *Arch. Journal* v (1848), p. 122, Rev. H. Hartshorne holds that the original roof was probably semicircular as at Hereford, but this seems unlikely. A tie-beam is more probable, resting on the sleeper wall as at present.

[2] MS. add. (Brit. Mus.), 14, 252, fol. 133 b. It is printed in Turner and Parker, p. 281.

[3] *Chronica Jocelini de Brakelonda*, Camden Soc. edit., 1840, p. 70.

[4] Harleian MSS. no. 603, fol. 57. Photograph in Lloyd, p. 4.

[5] Seen in the treforium at Christchurch Priory. Shingles were apparently used in the chief hall of Brionne Castle—destroyed in 1090 by fire as a result. (Ordericus Vitalis : *Historia Ecclesiastica*, ed. A. le Prévost, iii, 341).

ARCADING

(1) *Nave arcades*

Timber was no doubt more often used than stone in the nave arcades of the aisled hall. This is suggested by the available evidence, and is not surprising considering the probable wooden origin of this type of house. The most perfect example, however, of such a Norman hall occurs at Oakham, where the usual construction has been translated into stone in the manner of ecclesiastical building.

The wooden halls at Hereford and Leicester had square piers, with, in the case of the former, attached shafts on each face, those on the nave side being visible at a higher level than the spring of the longitudinal arcades. According to Mr. T. H. Fosbrooke's reconstruction Leicester aisled hall had no true arcade, but instead a construction familiar to us in medieval barns, with tall posts supporting braced purlins and tie beams. This form may have been frequent, and seems typologically earlier, although it lasted into modern times for use in farm-buildings.

(2) *Wall arcading—Dais arcades*

There is evidence of wall arcading at the upper end of the hall of Wolvesey, Bishop's Waltham and St. Mary's Guild. In the two former the arches are slightly pointed, in the latter semicircular and larger.

Window arcades

At Pudsey's Hall at Durham, there is an elaborate system of wall arcading remaining in connection with the 'triforium' windows to south and west. No doubt it also existed originally on the north wall. The scheme consists of high rear-arches to the windows, flanked by two smaller arches on the wall space between, all the arcade being enriched with double chevron. The arches are supported by shafts with bases on a plinth common to each section of the wall, and are tied to the wall surface by elongated capitals or imposts. Somewhat similar was the original arrangement at Westminster, here in connection with a wall-passage and probably such a scheme was not uncommon in the larger Norman halls.

External wall arcading occurs in Sherborne Castle at first-floor level. The round arches are interlaced and supported on columns with bases resting on a string-course.

FLOORS

There is very little evidence about the floors of Norman houses, for most have been replaced. In basements the floor was probably one merely of rammed earth, and in the first-floor hall either wooden or stone with regard to the method of roofing the basement. Where that was vaulted the hall had a stone floor, as at Boothby Pagnell, where the original probably remains, but there is a possibility that wood may have been superimposed on the stone in some cases. Certainly wooden floors occurred in the unvaulted halls at Richmond and Christchurch, where the floor itself has gone, but joist-holes for it remain on the side walls. At King John's House the joists were apparently supported by a ledge some 9 in. wide. There is no evidence for or against the existence of a 'dais.'

CHIMNEYS

(1) *The Cylindrical Chimney Type* consists of a cylindrical chimney-shaft[1] supported from below by a flat buttress on the outside wall. Two examples remain.[2]

(2) *The Buttress Type.* It may be that these are but the mutilated remains of the first type of chimney, for, as we have seen, the buttress formed a necessary means of support for the cylindrical shaft.[3] On the other hand, the smoke may have found an outlet in vents on the buttress just below the eaves. In every case the buttresses have been decapitated, so it is impossible to say.

[1] Conical caps, if they existed, have now disappeared.

[2] Christchurch; Boothby Pagnell; and probably originally at King John's House.

[3] It also thickened the wall to contain the fireplace.

However that may be, we have in some of these buttress examples an ingenious device absent in houses where the cylindrical shaft remains intact. In the two Jew's Houses at Lincoln, the buttress does not reach the ground, but is supported on the deeply projecting hood-mould of the entrance doorway, which in this case is on the ground-floor. This might indeed be an argument against the former existence here of a cylindrical chimney, as its weight might force the hood-mould out of shape; although the King John's House example, also with a partial buttress, if it indeed belongs to type (1), might prove that a full length buttress was unnecessary to support a tall chimney-shaft.

FIREPLACES

Probably the first-floor hall had a wall fireplace, the ground-floor hall a central hearth. This is the usual and most probable theory with regard to early medieval houses. Later the wall fireplace became common everywhere, with a few exceptions, one of which is the Great Hall at Hampton Court in which the central hearth occurs on the first floor, but certainly over a thick brick vault. In the twelfth century we know of no such example of daring, even in the case where the basement was vaulted below, and the first-floor hall seems to have possessed, from its very character, the wall fireplace.[1]

Indeed it is only in first-floor halls that fireplaces exist at all in Norman houses. With regard to the ground floor we have only negative evidence, which, together with the fact that floors in general have been renewed, may seem to support the theory of the open hearth. This was apparently in the centre of the room, with an opening in the roof to allow the escape of smoke. It is not known what happened in a ground-floor apartment when another storey overhead prevented the smoke from passing out that way. Either such a room, used for storage and offices, was not

[1] It has been suggested that the first-floor hearth might have been placed above one of the basement columns.

heated, the cooking being performed in an adjoining building possibly of timber, or the smoke from an open hearth found its way out as best it could. Blackened beams in the 'lower hall' at Luddesdown suggest this, although Mr. Cobbett Barker also claims to have found a wall fireplace there. In any case this is a dubious example with regard to date, and there is no definite evidence in other basements more certainly Norman.[1]

Original fireplaces are visible in four houses. They date to the second half of the twelfth century, and fall into two types, an earlier and a later.

(1) *The Arched Fireplace*[2] has a round or segmental arch in line with the wall or in a slight projection from it. This arch is supported by jamb-shafts, and the recess behind is approximately semicircular in plan.

(2) *The Hooded Fireplace* seems to belong to the transitional period into Early English. Indeed it is the type prevalent until the fifteenth century. The hood projects into the room, and is supported on corbels, while there is less need for a deep recess into the wall. However, our evidence depends on a single example, the fireplace at Boothby Pagnell (c. 1200).

WINDOWS

In basements loops are general, with two-light windows in the hall above. For ground-floor halls we have little evidence, but the one-light window does occur.

Loops were of defensive character, also the basement, largely used for storage, did not require good lighting. There are several varieties of loop,[3] with round or square heads, occasionally recessed in the wall, and always deeply splayed internally.

In the hall the *two-light window* is normal. It has a mid-shaft or mullion and frequently jamb-shafts in one or more recessed orders. Examples can be divided into types based on the number of shafts on the external face.

[1] A round-arched recess on the ground-floor at West Malling may be a fireplace (it is now a cupboard), and there was possibly one at Eynsford.

[2] King John's House; Hemingford Grey; Christchurch.

[3] Scolland's Hall; Sherborne; Christchurch; St. Mary's Guild.

The one-shaft window is probably earliest, met with in houses up to c. 1150;[1] it has a mid-shaft only and no covering arch, the two lights being flush with the outer wall.

The three-shaft window is found c. 1150–60.[2] Here there is, in addition to the mid-shaft, one jamb-shaft a side supporting an enclosing arch, of which the impost is sometimes extended to the shaftless inner order. This type occurs predominantly in the middle period of English Romanesque, and both orders and hood-mould are often richly decorated, especially with chevron.

The five-shaft window is also of two orders, but now with jamb-shafts to the lights as well, where they serve to balance the mid-shaft. There is a common impost in each jamb. The chevron now is less popular, although it appears luxuriantly at Durham (c. 1170), probably the earliest of our four examples.[3] In others varieties of deep roll and groove mouldings are preferred, sometimes with ball and acanthus ornament.[4]

The five-shaft window is an elaboration of the three-shaft type. It may be due to greater wealth on the part of the owner, two of the houses in which such windows occur belonging by tradition to Jews, or, and this seems more probable, the type may be a natural development from the three-shaft window.

With regard to the theory of greater wealth, it may be noted that many three-shaft windows have more elaborate carving than these, for instance the north window at Christchurch, and the elaborate outer order at Saltford.

On the other hand, the typological view is supported by three lines of argument. (1) Five-shaft windows occur in houses dated by their ornament to a period later than those in which three-shaft windows are found. The number of examples is small, but it is curious to note that the last three-shaft we have is

[1] Scolland's Hall; King John's House; Portslade (E. Window).

[2] Saltford; Christchurch.

[3] Durham; Jew's House; Aaron's House; Charleston.

[4] Internal jambs are straight in the one-shaft window; in the three-shaft either splayed or straight at first, then splayed to meet the lights; and splayed in the five-shaft type.

dated c. 1160 (Christchurch), while the four houses with five-shaft windows were built around the years 1170–80. (2) The three-shaft window at Saltford (c. 1150) contains the germ of this later type, in its attached quarter shafts,[1] apparently a development from the roll of earlier windows. At Christchurch the impost of the outer order capital is continued to the shaftless inner jamb, and even at King John's House, where no jamb-shafts existed, the jambs have imposts to balance the abacus of the mid-shaft. It would therefore be natural to complete the design by the addition of jamb-shafts and capitals to the inner order. (3) Such a growth in the size of the window would be expected, especially when settled times became more normal, and houses be expected to last longer intact. It is curious, however, that the size of the individual lights does not seem to have much increased.

Other types include the two-light of one order with a mullion instead of mid-shaft,[2] and two-lights of the Transition period.[3] The latter denote a return to an earlier simplicity, having fewer jamb-shafts, or sometimes only a mid-shaft. The straight head now occurs, and there are sometimes internal jamb-shafts.

One-light windows are found occasionally. Two[4] are in bad condition externally, thus it is not impossible that they are mutilated two-lights. However, at Sherborne, the one-light form is certain in two good windows, one of which has rich chevron decoration, also jamb-shafts in the outer order.

Of ground-floor hall windows, few examples remain: in the aisled hall both one and two-light forms occur,[5] and the one-light type seems probable in the unaisled hall.[6]

SHUTTERS

There is no evidence of the use of glass, but many of the mullions and jambs are rebated, probably for

[1] Or rather half-shafts, for the other quarter shows internally.

[2] Hemingford Grey; Portslade (S. window).

[3] Moyse's Hall; Merton Hall; Boothby Pagnell.

[4] West Malling; Canute's Palace.

[5] Leicester; Oakham.

[6] Minster; Horton Court; Sutton Courtenay.

shutters. At King John's House peg-holes remain in the mullion.

WINDOW SEATS

Stone window-seats and a raised foot-rest are a feature in two late examples. No doubt other houses had the same originally, but the sills in most cases have been altered beyond recognition. Fortunately the two we have are in excellent condition. The seats have a roll edge at Moyse's Hall, but at Boothby Pagnell the under-edge is chamfered like an impost. At the former the seats are parallel with the splayed jambs, in the latter at right angles to the wall.

It may be mere chance that the surviving Norman examples are late, but on the other hand the possibility of a late twelfth-century development of this kind is supported by the fact that the window-seat continued, hardly altered, into the thirteenth and fourteenth centuries. Henry III called them 'well-sitting windows,'[1] and where the lights were high, something of the sort was necessary in order to see out.[2]

DOORWAYS

Doorways are rebated and generally round-headed. Segmental[3] and shouldered[4] arches, however, do occur, and a slight point can be seen in the entrance to St. Mary's Guild. The outer arch is sometimes lower than the rear-arch, and the inner jambs are straight or slightly splayed. Beyond the rebate the doorway is often divided into recessed orders, with shafts in the jambs. Two orders are usual, but three occur at Appleton, and three large with two smaller in the great doorway at Durham. At Farnham the jamb-shafts and decoration are found on the inner face. Simpler doorways without shafts are often finished with chamfered edges or a roll-

[1] Liberate Roll—29, Henry III.

[2] At Christchurch the window recesses are carried to floor level, with a wide sill to the lights.

[3] Segmental outer arches are found at Farnham, Christchurch (S. doorway). Segmental rear arches are found at Saltford, Farnham, and Appleton.

[4] Boothby Pagnell hall cellar has a shouldered outer arch with a joggled segmental arch within.

moulding. Bar holes still exist at Scolland's Hall, and Chilham, Luddesdown and Sutton Courtenay.

STAIRCASES

Staircases were apparently a usual feature in Norman houses, although, judging from manuscripts, ladders with trap-doors were much used in the early Middle Ages for internal communication. This was the case even in royal dwellings of the thirteenth century. Henry III's injunctions to his bailiffs make reference to them,[1] and illustrated documents show servants ascending by interior ladders presumably from the offices to a first-floor hall.[2] Such a means of approach, now destroyed, may solve the problem of how the basement and hall were connected, when apparently the hall had but one door, and that the main entrance. But this does not seem to have been the method in a vaulted basement such as exists at Boothby Pagnell.

Sometimes, however, a newel stair would provide communication between the floors. This is found at Chilham, Richmond, Christchurch and Durham. Such stairs usually occur at the angles of the building, and may have been contained in a square turret of slight projection.[3]

In first-floor halls an outer entrance stairway was essential, but unfortunately none survive. No doubt they were often timber structures, but stone ones probably occurred. An entrance stair at Merton was repaired in 1375, and existed in the eighteenth century.

Such stairs seem to have ascended either parallel to the walls, or at right angles to it, the former being more compact and usual in castles, for they could be flanked by the hall windows. At Boothby Pagnell the stairway seems to have been at right angles to the building, and on the site of the modern one, for no marks on the east wall suggest a flanking stair.

[1] There was even a 'trapa descendens' in the chapel at Clarendon (Liberate Roll, 28, Henry III).

[2] B.M.MS. Cott. Nero C iv, photograph in Hartley and Elliott, *The People's Life and Work Series*, i, Pl. 4 (b).

[3] Chilham; Christchurch (see reconstruction in Quennell, *Everyday Life in Saxon, Danish and Norman Times* (1926), p. 97).

A covered stair open at the sides is suggested at Durham, where the entrance arch is especially elaborate and well preserved.[1] A contemporary staircase of this type survives at Canterbury,[2] where the roof is supported on columns, and the open arcading resembles the treatment of a refectory pulpit stair. This, the most important, if not the only external twelfth-century stair surviving, belongs to the type which descends away from the wall, but is elaborated by a right-angled turn at the bottom.

Wall Passages occurred originally at Westminster Hall and King John's House, and traces of one can still be seen at Wolvesey.

AUMBREYS AND LAMP-STANDS

Original recesses are sometimes found in the interior walls.[3] These were probably used as aumbreys (or cupboards) or lamp stands. The first use is probable when the openings are rebated for a door now destroyed. They have square or triangular heads.

SANITARY CONTRIVANCES

No traces remain, save for the garderobes at Richmond and Christchurch, which are additions. But no doubt there was some primitive form originally[4]; there is evidence of such in thirteenth-century houses,[5] and well planned rere-dorters occur even in Norman monasteries.[6]

MOATS

Moats, now dry, remain at Nytimber, Hemingford Grey, Appleton (three sides) and Boothby Pagnell. At Bishop's Waltham the moat is wet on the north side.

[1] *V.C.H. Durham*, iii, 81.

[2] Stairway to the Almonry. Photograph in Lloyd, p. 297.

[3] King John's House (2), Boothby Pagnell (2), Aaron the Jew's House.

[4] Jocelin de Brakelond gives a hint of something of the kind, at the Abbot's Grange of Warkton (Camden Soc. edition, p. 23).

[5] e.g. Stokesay Castle, Shropshire. See Lloyd, p. 472, for illustration. Also documentary evidence in the Liberate Rolls (e.g. 36 Henry III), and Close Rolls (e.g. 30, Henry III).

[6] e.g. Lewes Priory — W. H. Godfrey, *Official Guide to Lewes*, p. 23.

MOULDINGS

(1) *Abaci and Imposts.* The groove and chamfered under-edge is constant in abaci and imposts, the hollow chamfer being the most popular form ; while in the Transitional period the mouldings were elaborated, often by the addition of rolls to the groove and hollow chamfer. Abaci are usually square in plan, sometimes polygonal.

(2) *String Courses* were a favourite method of decoration and used both inside and out. Externally they divided up the elevation horizontally, and usually run in close association with the windows, at sill or impost level, in the latter carried as a hood mould round the arch.

Internal string-courses occur in relation to the window-seats, and connect the window recesses. Few, however, remain.

The chamfered under-edge is common, with sometimes the upper-edge as well ; roll mouldings are also found, while richly ornamented strings occur at Jew's House and St. Mary's Guild.

(3) *Arch Mouldings.* Semicircular hood-moulds are frequent, usually chamfered and often with ornament on the under-edge. A common arch moulding is the angle roll flanked by hollows, but it was often replaced by carved ornament of which the chevron was most popular.

(4) *Bases.* The most usual type is the crude attic base, consisting of a hollow between two roll-mouldings, the lower being the larger and flatter. Some of the earlier houses retain the vertical line of early Norman bases, but most examples show a sloping profile.

ORNAMENT

(*a*) *Capitals.* The scallop capital is typical of the first half, the foliated of the second half of the twelfth century. Of the latter two varieties can be separated : the palm-leaf capital with a single row of long leaves curved slightly outwards ; and the volute capital which comes nearer to the classic Corinthian, having angle crockets or volutes rising above a row of wider leaves.

Of this almost identical examples are found in the doorway of Jew's House (1170–80), the windows at Moyse's Hall (c. 1180) and at Oakham (c. 1190). In the latter hall remarkable capitals occur in the nave, probably due to French influence, and about the same date is an admirable wing or acanthus capital recently discovered at St. Mary's Guild. Another variety of enriched capital is found at Charleston, and others with animal carving in the great doorway at Durham. The mutilated capitals at Canute's Palace and at Merton suggest late twelfth-century foliage of a more delicate character, perhaps developing towards the Early English stiff-stalk of the Appleton doorway.

(*b*) *Corbels* are various, and the most remarkable are again found at Oakham.

(*c*) *Types of Ornament.* The chevron is the most popular ornament especially in the florid period of Romanesque, c. 1130–1175. It is used either out-turned or parallel with the wall surface. Although the single chevron is found, the double form is more common, probably due to the comparatively late date of most surviving houses. Other forms include the pellet, recessed panel, and acanthus, as well as the nail-head which later developed into dog-tooth. At Jew's House there is an uncommon design of interlaced or basket pattern, and the string-course at St. Mary's Guild is also remarkable. No richly-carved tympana survive in Norman dwelling-houses, but the window tympana at Oakham are decorated with sunk arches, arcading or a heart-shaped foliage.

(*d*) *Figure Sculpture* is chiefly found in the last period of the Norman house. Carved heads of men and women were popular, also grotesques and small figure pieces, for corbels, finials, and spandril ornaments. The workmanship is generally crude except at Oakham, which indeed furnishes most examples.

DETAILS

Wall Treatment

Walls may have been plastered externally, or whitewashed on the analogy of the White Tower of

London. But no signs of such a treatment remain.[1] The latter is also true of the internal face of the walls, coated as they are with modern plaster or wall-paper. No doubt these were plastered originally and painted with sham masonry joints or designs in primary colours. Some twelfth-century churches[2] retain such decoration, but in a much more elaborate form than would have been the case in domestic buildings.[3]

Henry III found plastered and painted walls in his palaces, and in some cases relined them with wainscot.[4] This was also coloured, and may have occurred even in the twelfth century. Tapestry was not general until well into the thirteenth century, but it is possible that the Normans had similar hangings to the woollen 'wall-cloths' of the Saxons.[5]

Furniture was scanty or crude in the Norman period, and doubtless consisted merely of a chair for the lord, benches, boards on trestles, and perhaps a chest. Illustrations of chairs,[6] and wooden beds[7] occur in contemporary MSS., but probably they were rarities, and only for important people. A bench, and the floor with or without a rough mattress would suffice for lesser folk.

THE NORMAN HOUSE IN RELATION TO THE TYPICAL MEDIEVAL HOUSE

No survey of twelfth-century dwelling-houses would be complete without some examination of the relation-

[1] Whitewash and plaster were a protection against fire. See Addy, *Evolution of the English House* (1933), p. 135. Turner and Parker (p. 11) quote the Bayeux Tapestry as evidence for coloured exteriors.

[2] Clapham, *English Romanesque Architecture: II. After the Conquest*, p. 146.

[3] A remnant of possibly twelfth-century painting remains on a beam above the wooden arch at Hereford. It consists of a series of white five-petalled flowers.

[4] Lloyd, p. 31, gives details.

[5] Wall coverings embroidered with gold are mentioned in '*Beowulf*' (lines 994–5). The Bayeux 'Tapestry,' however, was rather embroidery consisting of pictures stitched in wool on a strip of linen 230 ft. long by 22 in. wide.

[6] See illustrations in Hartley and Elliot, I, *The People's Life and Work Series* (eleventh to thirteenth centuries). Plate 2 (e) eleventh-century 'X' stool with claw feet (B.M. MS. Harl, 603). Plate 35 (a), twelfth-century rush chair with circular back, 'Bishop writing in basket chair.' (B.M. MS. Cott., Dom. XII). Turner and Parker, opposite p. 16 Seats in Bayeux Tapestry, ante p. 17, Table on trestles, M.S. Arch. A.154, Bodleian.

[7] Turner and Parker, opposite p. 14, illustrations of Romanesque beds, *Benedictional of St. Ethelwold and Caedmon* MS.

ship between the Norman domestic building, and what has been called the 'typical medieval house.' The latter is one having an H-type of plan,[1] and consisted of a lofty ground-floor hall two storeys high but open to the roof, with at each end projecting wings divided into floors and roofed separately from the hall. The 'upper-end chambers' or wing next to the dais normally contained a solar over a cellar, parlour or bower, access to which was obtained from the hall by a doorway and staircase near the high table. The 'lower-end' wing contained the offices and access to the kitchen, with later a private bed-chamber above corresponding to the solar. These rooms were reached from the hall by means of the 'entry,' a passage partitioned off from the main body of the hall by the wooden 'screens.' The latter sheltered the hall from draughts from the entrance doorway, which was placed in the main wall at right angles to the 'screens.' There was often another door opposite the entrance, and in the 'screens' openings corresponding to the two or three doorways opposite which led to buttery, pantry and kitchen. The 'entry' contained a ladder or newel stair communicating with a gallery above and thence to rooms over the offices.

Professor Hamilton Thompson even suggests that this type of medieval house occurred as early as the eleventh century. He quotes from a passage in Ordericus Vitalis,[2] describing how William Rufus and the later Henry I were playing dice 'upon the solar' in a house in the castle of l'Aigle. Their game created an uproar culminating in horse-play and the pouring of water on to the heads of Robert of Normandy and his men who were below, apparently outside the house. Robert then rushed into the dining-hall to retaliate. The Professor believes that the game was actually played in the solar or private chamber, but, as he

[1] R.C.H.M. Essex, IV, XXXV.

[2] Ordericus Vitalis: *Historia Ecclesiastica*, ed. A. le Prévost. Paris, 1838–55, vol. ii, p. 295. 'Unde in Aquilensi castro ad hospitium Rodberti, quod in domo Rogerii Calcegii susceperat, venerunt, ibique super solarium (sicut militibus moris est) tesseris ludere coeperunt. Deinde ingentem strepitum fecere, et aquam super Rodbertum et asseclas ejus, qui subtus erant, fudere. . . . His siquidem auditis furibundus surrexit, et in coenaculum contra fratres suos virepere acceleravit.'

admits, 'solarium' is also a general term for any room above ground-level, and the brothers may have been playing in a first-floor hall. This seems to be the more probable explanation, otherwise why is it only described how Robert rushed into the dining-hall? If a typical medieval plan was in view, he would not only have to cross the hall, but also climb up the stairs to the solar at its upper end. He is described merely as entering the hall, and this suggests that he rushed up the external staircase and found his brothers at play in a hall on the first-floor such as we find at Christchurch, Boothby Pagnell, and the eleventh-century Scolland's Hall at Richmond.

Although the H. type of house seems later than the twelfth century, Romanesque prototypes probably existed. Of the three forms of Norman house, it has naturally most in common with the unaisled ground-floor hall. If the latter were prototype, we might expect to find in remaining examples a suggestion of the later 'entry,' probably not yet divided off by screens, and also some hint of projecting cross-wings. The former is given by the arrangement of the north and south doorways at Horton and Sutton Courtenay; while at Appleton we have a typical 'entry' but for the absence of screens. This house, dating c. 1210, may be transitional in plan as it is in style, and link the simple halls of Horton (c. 1140) and Sutton Courtenay (c. 1190) with the developed medieval type of the thirteenth, fourteenth and fifteenth centuries.

But for Appleton, however, there are no indications of incipient cross-wings, perhaps of timber; indeed at Sutton Courtenay an original west window forbids any but a low outbuilding at that end, and we have already noted the suggestion of an annexe at right angles to the hall on the north.

The aisled hall might equally well be the prototype, and probably was; aisles were found in many thirteenth-century houses, but disappeared almost entirely before the end of the fourteenth century, probably owing to more scientific roof development which allowed an undivided floor space. In thirteenth-century houses, later additions have often made away with the timber posts of the aisles, and this may even have been the case with Appleton. Horton and Sutton Courtenay, being narrow buildings, did not require this triple method of roofing. At Oakham (c. 1190) the stone piers remain, and here blocked doorways in the east wall indicate lower-end chambers on both floors, but not so high as to interfere with the gable window.

But few Norman instances can be quoted in the case of either ground-floor hall, and the matter is chiefly one of probability.

It might even be considered that the first-floor hall was the prototype, or rather its developed hall-and-solar form. The hall might have descended to ground-level when defence was no longer urgent, while the solar remained on an upper floor over its basement.

The chief argument against the idea is shown by the thirteenth and fourteenth-century development of the first-floor hall. Here instead of the cross-wings of the typical medieval house, subsidiary buildings, now of stone, project certainly at right angles but usually off the side and not the end walls of the hall. Little Wenham Hall, Suffolk,[1] is a typical example of this arrangement, the hall and chapel blocks forming an L-type of plan. A more curious variety occurs at Old Soar, Plaxtol, Kent,[2] where the solar and chapel just touch the corners of the hall, somewhat like three playing-cards connected only at the angles. On the other hand, it might be urged that Aydon Castle Hall[3] has a solar cross-wing like part of the typical plan, as is the case at the fourteenth-century Markenfield Hall;[4] also that in some ground-floor halls the cross-wings project very little, like the north wing at Sutton Courtenay Manor-house,[5] or give place to outbuildings

[1] Lloyd, pp. 178–180.

[2] Lloyd, pp. 180–181. But is this 'hall' really a solar, with chapel and garderobe? If so, the hall was probably on the site of the modern range; it would be of ground-floor type, communicating with the solar basement.

[3] Lloyd, p. 182. Quennell, *A History of Everyday Things in England* i, 76. These three examples date to the thirteenth century.

[4] Markenfield Hall is near Ripon, Yorkshire. See Lloyd, p. 185. It is more like an L-type of plan, with the hall as the shorter arm.

[5] This dates to the fourteenth century, is now called 'The Abbey,' and must not be confused with the earlier 'Norman hall' in the same village. The solar is reached by an external stair, this feature occurring also at the thirteenth-century Charney Basset. For these see Parker ii, 272, and Fletcher, p. 396 respectively.

off the side wall of the hall, Cottesford Manor-house, Oxfordshire,[1] being an example. Thus the evidence is not conclusive.

More probable is the theory that the first-floor hall was ancestor only to the two-storeyed block of solar over vaulted basement, and that the medieval house was evolved out of both ground and first-floor halls, combining the good points of each.

The advantages of the first-floor hall lay in the fact that it was more economical of material, more compact[2] and defensive, and that it allowed cellar accommodation and larger windows than would have been feasible on ground-level in times of unrest. Its defensive character was the one to appeal most to the medieval mind, but would lessen in importance as the country grew more settled, and in periods of quiet there were many inconveniences in the first-floor hall. Perhaps the chief was the length of time it took to carry dishes from an outside kitchen to the hall either by ladders in the basement, or up the entrance stairway, for we have no evidence that the cellars were used for cooking in the twelfth century.

Thus as the medieval period advanced, the first-floor hall declined in importance. In stone halls of the twelfth century it was normal, in the thirteenth it was perhaps equalled by the numbers of ground-floor halls, less than these in the fourteenth, and a rarity in the fifteenth century. However, as it was still an advantage to have a strong basement for storage, that feature was borrowed, and the upper end of the medieval house may represent the old hall and cellar arrangement incorporated in a larger scheme.

More than a hint of this development is given by certain houses which comprise two periods of building; a thirteenth-century solar, and a fourteenth- or fifteenth-century ground-floor hall. This would suggest that when more room was required, a larger

[1] Turner and Parker, p. 162. This is a thirteenth-century building.

[2] But compactness was not a medieval quality in housing; even royal palaces being a series of buildings loosely tacked together and added to when required. Probably if we could see the first-floor hall as it used to be, flanked by various outbuildings of timber, its compact nature would be far less obvious.

hall was added, now safely on the ground, and the earlier first-floor hall retained as its solar. Such was apparently the case in the Parsonage House at West Tarring, where a thirteenth-century hall became solar to a later hall at right angles to it.[1] The Prebendal House at Thame is more complicated; here the thirteenth-century hall had a solar and chapel projecting west and east at its southern end. All three were built on basements, and the fifteenth-century hall was added to the north, with a new two-storeyed block at the farther end next the screens.[2]

Yet if such was the line of development, by the fourteenth century the sub-solar basement had lost its vaulting, and become the parlour or bower, another private room probably a chamber for the women of the household, while it was considered more convenient to have the storage accommodation next to the offices at the lower end of the hall. That lower wing was being extended, for progress in standards of living not only demanded more private bedrooms but also an increase in service accommodation.

Arguments against this inclusion, into the H-type of house, of the hall and cellar arrangement may well be found, not only in the rapid transformation of cellar into parlour or bower, but also in the fact that halls of first-floor type continued to be built contemporaneous with examples of its adoption into the larger plan. But it is well known in typology how earlier forms survive side by side with derivative types, and in building conservatism, individual taste and local conditions combine to produce a variety of dwellings borrowing features from each other. The size of the house is another factor, and the H-type was suitable for larger buildings, while for smaller houses it was general to adopt the L-plan often found in first-floor halls. The evolution of the medieval house is a complicated matter, but on the whole that house seems to have been developed from a combina-

[1] *Sussex Arch. Collections*, lxiv (1923), pp. 140–179, with plan and illustrations (A. B. Packham).

[2] *Arch. Journal*, lxvii (1910), pp. 367–9.

tion of the aisled ground-floor hall with features found convenient in the first-floor type of house.

ADDENDA

CHIMNEYS The word chimney (*caminum*) in medieval documents meant the whole heating structure including the fireplace. Here, however, we are concerned with 'chimney' in its modern sense of the flue outlet or shaft alone.

The earliest type of Norman chimney surviving is found in early twelfth-century keeps. Here the smoke outlets are contrived in the side of a shallow buttress by means of oblong vents. Of this Castle Hedingham (c. 1130) provides a good example: the south buttress contains flues for fireplaces at two levels, though the side outlets have been blocked. The contemporary keep at Rochester has a similar arrangement, as also London, Colchester and Canterbury earlier. The late Hugh Braun showed that the presence of two vents, one on each side of a flat buttress, would enable the windward vent to be closed in heavy weather, the leeward one being thus assisted, through the protection of the buttress, to 'draw' more efficiently.[1] He noted that only in later twelfth-century keeps such as Scarborough (1158–64) do the flues ascend vertically through the wall. In houses they probably discharged under the eaves.

Circular draught holes running obliquely through the back wall are found in twelfth-century fireplaces at the keeps of Tretower (Brecon) and Ogmore (Glamorgan). At Ogmore the series of holes at the back of the flue are about a foot above the level of the chimney breast.[2] In the keep at Portchester (Hampshire), c. 1160 to before 1172, on the first floor, the northern fireplace has a flue rising some 10 ft. up the wall to a domed vault, and narrow slits in the wall let out the smoke.[3] The angle kitchen at Castle Rising has a similar dome to a circular flue 5 ft. 6 in. in diameter, and loop-hole vents[4] like the larger one 8 ft. 10 in. in diameter at Canterbury, rising 20 ft. up, with loop outlets for the flues in the angle with the buttresses.[5]

By the middle of the twelfth century the cylindrical chimney had appeared, and may have been common in stone houses. The earliest surviving examples yet known are found at Framlingham Castle. Two chimneys serving the hall block of c. 1150–60 are incorporated in the late twelfth-century curtain wall, and have

[1] H. Braun, *The English Castle* (1936), p. 29. For plan and sections of this arrangement at Colchester, see S. Toy, *The Castles of Great Britain* (1953), p. 161.

[2] *M.O.W. guide* (C. A. R. Radford, 1956), p. 7.

[3] *M.O.W. guide* (The late Sir Charles Peers, 1957), p. 8. Toy. op. cit., p. 86.

[4] Toy. op cit., p. 84. The flue over the dome is probably later.

[5] Toy, op. cit., p. 73 (plan), 74.

round-headed lancet vents, Tudor brick extensions probably replacing a conical cap. At Christchurch Castle the hall of c. 1160 has a simple shaft supported by a flat buttress with shallow offsets on the external wall. Occasionally the buttress does not reach ground level as at King John's House, Southampton (c. 1150) where a cylindrical chimney once existed, and the same is true of the two Jew's Houses at Lincoln (c. 1170–80) here supported on the projecting hood-mould of the entrance doorway.[1] At Boothby Pagnell (c. 1200) the chimney resembles that at Christchurch, but has a gabled buttress. A contemporary chimney at Southampton was removed from the bombed house, 79½ High Street, and re-set in the somewhat earlier King John's House: here the thistle-profile cap is original, while those of Christchurch and Boothby Pagnell may be somewhat restored.

At the present stage of our knowledge we may assume two types of the twelfth-century chimney shaft: the cylindrical chimney with open top, and that with side vents and conical capping. It might be argued that the first type is a vestigial example of the second, which has lost its conical cap. The edging at Christchurch may be restored, and this can be visualised with a lantern stage and conical cap as in the remarkable shaft called 'La Lanterne des Morts' at Bayeux. The same may have occurred at Boothby Pagnell; but at Southampton, the High Street chimney preserves its original thistle-like top, and this splayed out over a waist-moulding makes a lantern cone unlikely here. At Framlingham we seem on firmer ground. The cylindrical chimneys are partly built up in later twelfth-century walling, but their tops are free and have four blunt lancet vents in the circumference below the Tudor brick. Compared with the late thirteenth-century chimney remaining at Aydon Castle, Northumberland, the resemblance is striking. Although the Aydon chimney is partly attached to the outer wall it has the same vents above a string-course, though here the lancets, being later, are pointed, and there are only two, while above is a conical cap which must have existed once at Framlingham.

At Old Sarum there is definite evidence, for parts of a large stone cylindrical chimney were found,[2] having one or two courses of circular smoke-holes below a chevron string-course, and confined by a band of scroll-pattern below: similar vents were pierced in the sloping stones apparently of a conical cap in the Bayeux manner. The French chimney, however, has a loftier cone or steeple with room for some ten rows of smoke-holes in its height.

FIREPLACES The ground-floor hall, two storeys high, seems to have been heated, as in the thirteenth and fourteenth centuries, by a central hearth, with an opening or louver in or near the roof to carry away the smoke. In a two-storeyed block the wall fireplace was

[1] A cylindrical chimney is shown in the reconstruction (with plan) of Jew's House in L. Veltheim Lottum, *Kleine Weltgeschichte des Städtischen Wohnhauses* (Heidelberg, 1952), pp. 216–17.

[2] Now in the Museum at Salisbury.

used as early as the late eleventh century; for a central hearth would have been inconvenient except in a lofty hall with room for the smoke to escape, while on an upper level it would have been dangerous without a solid floor of stone or above a pier of the vaulted undercroft. However, a portable iron brazier of charcoal may have been generally used for heating.

Just as the central hearth dates its ancestry from the earliest type of fireplace which warmed the caves and huts of primitive man, and is now represented by the bonfire, so the wall fireplace was probably the next development when it was found convenient to build the fire against a wall or shorter reredos, and thus enable a pot to be hung from a horizontal bar attached to the back. Then a funnel or hood was invented to collect and control the smoke, and the next stage was to set the hearth back into a stone wall, in which the funnel was incorporated. In Norman keeps such as Colchester and Canterbury, vents were made on either side of a fireplace buttress, or thickened wall, and which could be regulated according to the direction of the wind.

The earliest Norman fireplaces were arched, such as the round-headed examples in the keeps at Colchester (c. 1090), Rochester (1126–39) and Castle Hedingham, Essex (c. 1130). At King John's House, Southampton (c. 1150) springers remain to show that the head was segmental, a shape used in the two warming-house fireplaces of the end of the twelfth century at Rievaulx Abbey, Yorkshire. Chevron was probably a favourite ornament for the arch; it is combined with mouldings at Rochester, and doubled at Castle Hedingham. The supporting jamb-shafts had cushion or scalloped capitals, which also survive at Hemingford Grey and King John's House. The semi-circular plan is usual, and the fireplace might be set in a slight projection, the walls being also thickened by means of an external buttress which supported the chimney. At Hedingham the cone-shaped flue discharged through two rectangular openings (now closed) flanking the central buttresses (S. wall) like the vents at Colchester and Canterbury keeps.

Towards the end of the twelfth century the hooded fireplace appeared, an improvement for the discharge of smoke, the hood projecting into the room, and allowing for a shallower recess. It has been shown[1] that the two earliest known examples of a hooded fireplace, at Conisborough Keep (c. 1180) in Yorkshire, occur where the circular plan of the room made an arched fireplace difficult to construct. Here a lintel was formed along a chord of the circle, and the resulting filling above assumed a hooded form. The stone hood, pyramidal in shape, has a moulded string-course and rests on a joggled lintel, the stones thus stepped to prevent slipping. At Conisborough these are supported by triple clustered shafts, but corbels often occur, as in the fine example at Boothby Pagnell (c. 1200) where the hood is vertical then slopes back near its summit. The hooded fireplace continued in fashion, gathering refinement into the thirteenth and early fourteenth centuries.

[1] L. A. Shuffrey, *The English Fireplace* (1912), p. 16.

A. APPLETON MANOR: SERVICE DOORWAYS

B. SUTTON COURTENAY: 'NORMAN HALL,' SOUTH DOORWAY

A. INTERIOR OF NORTH WALL

B. WEST WALL AND FOURTEENTH-CENTURY ARCADE
KING JOHN'S HOUSE, SOUTHAMPTON

PLATE III.

A. CHRISTCHURCH CASTLE HALL: EAST FRONT

B. BOOTHBY PAGNELL MANOR HOUSE: CHIMNEY ON WEST WALL

A. ST. MARY'S GUILD, LINCOLN: WEST FRONT

B. BISHOP'S WALTHAM PALACE: SOUTH TOWER FROM NORTH-WEST

A. JEW'S HOUSE, LINCOLN: SOUTH FRONT

B. AARON THE JEW'S HOUSE, LINCOLN: VIEW FROM SOUTH-WEST

A. EAST FRONT

B. SOUTH WINDOWS (THE EASTERN IS INSERTED)
BOOTHBY PAGNELL MANOR HOUSE

A. BOOTHBY PAGNELL MANOR HOUSE: HALL CELLAR, LOOKING NORTH

B. MOYSE'S HALL, BURY ST. EDMUND'S: EASTERN BASEMENT

A. KING JOHN'S HOUSE, SOUTHAMPTON: FIREPLACE

B. BOOTHBY PAGNELL MANOR HOUSE: HALL FIREPLACE

A. SOUTH WINDOW B. WEST WINDOW

HEMINGFORD GREY MANOR HOUSE

C. CHRISTCHURCH CASTLE HALL: NORTH WINDOW

D. SALTFORD MANOR HOUSE: NORTH WINDOW

A. MOYSE'S HALL, BURY ST. EDMUNDS; HALL WINDOWS

B. CANUTE'S PALACE, SOUTHAMPTON: INTERIOR OF SOUTH WINDOW

C. BOOTHBY PAGNELL MANOR HOUSE: SOLAR WINDOW-SEATS

A. APPLETON MANOR ; DETAIL OF ENTRANCE

B. HEREFORD : GREAT HALL OF THE BISHOPS.
TIMBER CAPITAL OF NAVE

A. ST. MARY'S GUILD, LINCOLN: DAIS CAPITAL

B. SOUTHAMPTON VAULT: LATE TWELFTH-CENTURY CORBEL

PLATE XIII.

A. JEW'S HOUSE, LINCOLN: ENTRANCE DOORWAY

B. ST. MARY'S GUILD, LINCOLN: ENTRANCE ARCH AND STRING-COURSE

BURTON AGNES OLD HALL, YORKSHIRE:
UNDERCROFT